Keys
to Spiritual
Growth

Keys
to Spiritual
Growth

John F. MacArthur, Jr.

FLEMING H. REVELL COMPANY
Old Tappan, New Jersey

Scripture quotations not otherwise identified are from the King James Version of the Bible.

Scripture quotations identified RSV are from the Revised Standard Version of the Bible, copyrighted 1946, 1952, © 1971 and 1973.

Scripture quotations identified NAS are from the New American Standard Bible, Copyright © THE LOCKMAN FOUNDATION 1960, 1962, 1963, 1968, 1971, 1972, 1973 and are used by permission.

Extract on "The Fizzie Principle" is from GOD'S WILL IS NOT LOST by John F. MacArthur, Jr., published by Victor Books, copyright 1973, SP Publications, Inc., Wheaton, Ill. Used by permission.

Library of Congress Cataloging in Publication Data
MacArthur, John F., Jr., date
  Keys to spiritual growth.

  1. Christian life—1960–   I. Title.
BV4501.2.M16   248'.4   75–40301
ISBN 0–8007–0777–X hb
ISBN 0–8007–5013–6 pwbk

TO
Matthew, Marcy, Mark, and Melinda,
my beloved children, whose spiritual growth
is my constant concern, and whose maturity
will be my highest earthly joy

Contents

Preface

Life results in growth. Spiritual life results in spiritual growth, or at least it should. Are you growing? If you are not, or if you are not satisfied with your rate of growth, this book is for you!

Be sure of this—God intends every Christian to grow to spiritual maturity. His Word commands us: "But grow in grace, and in the knowledge of our Lord and Saviour Jesus Christ . . ." (2 Peter 3:18). That's our obligation—and our privilege. Each day we can progress in our spiritual life toward a fuller, higher, personal, experiential knowledge of God and Christ. We can go past His Word to the God who wrote it, and know Him more personally. But, I find that many people entertain mistaken ideas about what this vital subject involves.

Spiritual growth has nothing to do with our position in Christ. God sees us in His Son as already perfect. We are complete in Him (Colossians 2:10). We have "all things that pertain unto life and godliness" (*see* 2 Peter 1:3). We are new creations (2 Corinthians 5:17).

Spiritual growth has nothing to do with God's favor. God doesn't like us better the more spiritual we become. Sometimes parents threaten their children, "If you do such and such, the Lord won't like you." How ridiculous! God's love for us is not conditional upon our behavior. At the time when we were "without strength, ungodly, sinners, and enemies" (*see* Romans 5:6–10), God showed His great love for us by sending His Son to die for our sins. God cannot love us more just because we grow.

Spiritual growth has nothing to do with time. It is not measured by the calendar. It is possible for a person to be a Christian for half a century and yet be a spiritual infant. *Time* magazine reported on a quiz given to college students who had attended Sunday school for years. According to them, Sodom and Gomorrah were lovers; the Gospels were written by Matthew, Mark, Luther, and John; Eve was created from an apple; and Jezebel was Ahab's jackass. Retired persons might do even worse!

Spiritual growth has nothing to do with knowledge. A person may have a lot of facts, a lot of information, but that can't be equated with spiritual maturity. Unless your knowledge results in conforming you to Christ, it is useless. It must be life-changing.

Spiritual growth has nothing to do with activity. Some folks think that the mature Christians are the busy ones. But busyness doesn't result in maturity nor can it be substituted for it. It may, in fact, even be a hindrance to what is really vital and important in the Christian life. Matthew 7 tells us of a group who will plead acceptance with Christ on the basis of their wonderful works. But He will cast them out. Busyness doesn't even result in salvation, let alone maturity.

Spiritual growth has nothing to do with prosperity. "Well, look how the Lord has blessed me," some people exclaim. "I've got so much money, and I have a wonderful house and a nice car and a secure job. You see how God has blessed me because I've honored Him?" Don't believe it. God may have allowed you to prosper—or you may even have forced it—but that is no mark of spiritual growth. (*See* 2 Corinthians 12:7–10.)

I define spiritual growth simply as matching up your practice with your position. Your position in Christ is perfect. It is an absolute. And now God wants you to reflect that position in your progressive experience, which is relative. Such growth is critical. Call it what you will: *following after righteousness* (1 Timothy 6:11); *being transformed* (Romans 12:2); *perfecting holiness* (2 Corinthians 7:1); *pressing toward the mark* (Philippians 3:14); or *being built up in the faith* (Colossians 2:7). This is the goal for every Christian.

And spiritual growth is not mystical, sentimental, devotional, psychological, or the result of clever secrets. It comes through understanding and practicing the principles that are given in the Word of God. Its boundless blessings are in a divine vault that is easily unlocked by a series of very unique keys. These keys are the theme of this book. Get ready to unlock the riches of God in Christ Jesus!

Keys
to Spiritual
Growth

The Master Key—
A Presupposition

This chapter began as one of the "keys." But the more I looked at it, the more I realized it was not really a chapter but a presupposition to all the other chapters.

One of the many statements which the Bible makes concerning itself is that the Word of God lives. "Being born again, not of corruptible seed, but of incorruptible, by the word of God, which liveth and abideth for ever" (1 Peter 1:23). Paul refers to the Bible as the word of life (Philippians 2:16). And the writer of Hebrews says that the Word of God is alive and powerful (Hebrews 4:12).

"In what way is the Word of God alive?" you ask. "I mean, I pick up my Bible and it doesn't do anything. It just sits there. How is it alive? Are the pages alive—or the ink or the leather?"

Well, let's look at what is not living—or, more properly at what is dying. Things in our world are dead and dying. Decay, destruction, corruption—these things surround us. Death is really the monarch of this world. The world is really nothing but a large cemetery with everybody on the way out. People like to say, "I'm living it up!" Actually, they're living it on the downside, for their bodies and their glory soon wither and fade away like the grass (1 Peter 1:24).

In contrast, the Bible is inexhaustible, inextinguishable, and life-giving. The death system of this world cannot touch it, remove its validity, deteriorate its reality, or decay its truth.

Beware! It's Alive.   *First, the Bible is alive in itself.* The Bible lives in its perennial freshness. In every generation and every age, every person who picks up the Bible finds it to be fresh and living. I've found that true in my own experience. A few years ago I thought that if I read a book of the Bible every day for thirty days in a row, I'd pretty well know what was in that particular book. I started with 1 John and then Colossians. But at the end of thirty days, I discovered that there were still things that I didn't know about each book, so I tacked on an additional month. But even after that I still didn't know those little books as I felt I should, so I read them again for another thirty days. Know what? These books still hold mysteries for me that I haven't even tapped. Every time I pick them up I get excited!

Another reason we say the Bible lives is because of its lack of obsolescence. Have you ever looked at your old high school or college textbooks? Most of them are obsolete. Science keeps making discoveries and continues to produce new books. But the Bible never gets out-of-date.

Also, the Bible lives—in that it discerns hearts. It has insight that shakes us up. Sometimes when I read the Bible I get so sick of myself that I can hardly stand it. The Bible is a sharp two-edged sword that discerns the thoughts and intents of the heart (Hebrews 4:12). It rips me wide open and reveals to me exactly what I am. That's why those who want to do something bad don't read it. They are found out. These are some of the reasons why we say the Word of God is alive of itself.

Second, the Bible is life-giving. It not only has life, it gives life. The highest power that a living thing has is the ability to reproduce itself. Our thoughts and our words cannot do that. We could talk all day and it wouldn't result in spiritual life for anyone. But the living Word of God reproduces life. James 1:18 says, "Of his own will begat he us with the word of truth. . . ." The Word of God does the job. The Holy Spirit uses the Word to bring about new birth. The only way to become a child of God is to be born by the Word, the seed of new life.

Consider the parable of the Sower in Luke 8. The Word of God is the seed scattered over the world. That which falls by the wayside is soon taken away by the devil, lest the people should believe and be saved. What is the one ingredient that people must believe to be saved? The Word. It gives life.

Another proof that the Word is critical in the process of regeneration may be demonstrated from John 6:63. "It is the spirit that quickeneth; the flesh profiteth nothing: the words that I speak unto you, they are spirit, and they are life." The Spirit of God used the Word of God to produce life.

A third thing—the Bible sustains spiritual life. Life demands food, and the Word of God is that food. Peter said, "As newborn babes, desire the [pure] milk of the word, that ye may grow thereby" (1 Peter 2:2).

Just as you could not live without milk when you were a little baby, so desire spiritual food that you may grow spiritually. After all, you tasted that the Lord was gracious at the time of your salvation (v. 3). Don't you think that the taste is still going to be sweet when you start to taste the Word? In other words, if you have put off the flesh of the world, if you have seen that the Word of God can make you alive, can sustain your life, can transform your life, then desire it. You have tasted the Word; now feed on it.

Many Christians do not strongly desire the Word. As a result they are emaciated, improperly nourished, suffering malnutrition. Elsewhere the Bible speaks of itself as sustenance: "Thy words were found, and I did eat them; and thy word was unto me the joy and rejoicing of mine heart . . ." (Jeremiah 15:16).

Paul reminds Timothy of the same thing, but from a slightly different angle. "If thou put the brethren in remembrance of these things, thou shalt be a good minister of Jesus Christ, nourished up in the words of faith and of good doctrine, whereunto thou hast attained" (1 Timothy 4:6). The nourishment of the believer is the Word of God. We need it as a baby needs milk, but we also need to grow up so that we can finally get at the meat.

A fourth reason why we say the Word of God lives is that it transforms life. Paul wrote to the Ephesians to be renewed in the spirit of their minds (Ephesians 4:23). And in Romans 12:2 the apostle said that the renewing of our minds is something that must happen in order to transform us. Even as believers, we need to let the Word change us. We are not perfect when we become believers. The Holy Spirit still has lots to do to mold us into Christ's likeness. Even after we come into God's family, the old mind with its habits of self-occupation, with its craving for sensation, with its desire for excitement, with its imagination and appetites for wrong or questionable things of life—all this must be displaced. How? By the Word of God.

Everybody wants to be more dedicated to Christ—to be all that God wants us to be. We struggle around and wonder how commitment may be accomplished. We make our dedications, our resolutions for Christ, and still just keep going around and around, always trying to discover the means of accomplishment.

Well, let me introduce you to the most fantastically beautiful thing imaginable. Second Corinthians 3:14 gives us the answer to transformed lives. Speaking of Israel, this verse tells us, "But their minds were blinded: for until this day remaineth the same veil untaken away in the reading of the old testament; which veil is done away in Christ." In other words, Israel is blinded today, so that it cannot understand the Gospel. But the passage goes on to say that someday the veil will be taken away (v. 16).

Now what about believers—Christians? Are we shut off from Christ? No! "But we all, with open face beholding as in a glass the glory of the Lord, are changed into the same image from glory to glory, even as by the Spirit of the Lord" (v. 18).

But how can we get changed? How do we become transformed to be like Christ? Very simply—as we stand face-to-face looking into the glory of Jesus Christ, we shall be changed into His image! As we take our eyes off ourselves and fix them on Jesus, the Spirit of God will do the changing. I can promise you as a testimony of Scripture that if you stand with your face in the Word of God—learning and beholding the glory of God— the Spirit of God will transform you into the image of Jesus Christ. That is the epitome of spiritual growth.

Face-Lifting.   It is just that simple. Yet so many Christians are trying to figure out some kind of shortcut to superspirituality. It doesn't exist. When we are willing to set our faces into the mirror of the Word of God to behold the glory of God, all we have to do is focus on His Word and the glory of Christ within His Word will suddenly begin to change us.

I can say that the greatest thing that ever happened in my life, next to my salvation, occurred when I learned to study the Word of God night and day. While I haven't arrived, by any stretch of the imagination, I have learned this—that the longer and more intensely and more devotedly I look into the face of Jesus Christ on the pages of Scripture, the more the Spirit of God changes my life into the image of His Son. Bible study has become the passion of my heart for my own life. There is nothing in this world that consumes me like the desire to communicate the Word. All good things come through it. If we desire to live, the Word of God makes us alive. If we desire to grow, the Word of God gives us growth. And if we desire to be changed, the Word of God can do it as we focus our attention on its pages.

Turn the Lock.   Let me suggest five specific things that you can do in order to use the master key. First, believe it. Many things and many people may invite your attention and allegiance, but make Peter's response yours: "Lord, to whom shall we go? thou hast the words of eternal life" (John 6:68). Believe the Bible. Take it as the revelation of God.

Second, study it. I hope that, like Apollos, you will be mighty in the Scriptures (Acts 18:24). When Jesus opened and explained the Scriptures to the two disciples on the way to Emmaus, they said, "Didn't our hearts burn within us?" (*see* Luke 24:32). When you study the Word, it should set your heart ablaze. And as you study the Scriptures, you can show yourself approved of God (2 Timothy 2:15).

A third suggestion—honor the Word. The citizens of Ephesus honored the statue of Diana because they thought it fell from Jupiter out of heaven. So they worshiped it—ugly, gross, and horrible as it was. But something entirely lovely has come down out of heaven from God—His precious Word—more valuable than gold or rubies (Proverbs 3:14, 15).

Fourth, along with honor, love the Word of God. Give it your time and attention as you would any other less-deserving object of affection. "O how love I thy law! it is my meditation all the day," said the Psalmist (119:97). Can *you* say that?

Fifth, and perhaps most important, obey the Word of God. Do what it says. The communication of God isn't optional—something to submit yourself to, if you feel like it. It's obligatory. The great revival in Nehemiah's day took place when men came to the priest and said, "Bring the book" (*see* Nehemiah 8:1). Revive your heart by letting the Word of God be the rule of your life.

These five suggestions let you use the master key which opens everything! And yet there are other keys, each one unlocking another treasure of spiritual growth. Each one is based on the Master Key—each one a principle from the Word.

1

The Master Purpose—
The Glory of God

If you were to go out on the street and ask ten people at random to name what they considered to be the greatest theme in all the world, you would get a variety of answers: Money. Love. Marriage. Sex. Freedom. Security. Status. Pleasure. Peace. Happiness.

But from God's viewpoint, there is only one answer. It is the greatest theme in all the world, in all the Word of God, in all the universe. It lies behind the reason for Creation, the reason for living the Christian life, the reason for everything God has done or will do.

Can you name it? The answer may be found in what is known as the shorter catechism—the question-and-answer format which has long been used in the history of the church to give religious instruction. Here's the first question: "What is the chief end of man?" And here's the answer: "The chief end of man is to glorify God and to enjoy Him forever." So the writers of the catechism revealed what they considered to be the basic information that a person ought to have—the fact that he is for God's glory and God is for his enjoyment.

Life's Major Goal.   The glory of God! Why is man on this earth? Why did God bother to redeem him? What is the purpose of life? How is all of Creation—so much of it presently corrupted and deformed—how is this going to turn out? For the glory of God. It is vital that we understand the biblical concept of God's glory.

Someone may object that we are basing too much on the catechism, even though the catechism is essentially doctrine based on Scripture. But the paramount importance of the glory of God is not simply a statement of somebody's idea. It is supported directly in the Word of God. For example, look at Psalms 16:8—"I have set the Lord always before me. . . . " That refers to giving God glory. In making this statement, David is saying, in essence, "In everything I do, my attention is given to God. All that I do, I accomplish with my focus riveted on God. It's for His glory and His honor and His will."

The result is expressed in verse 9: "Therefore my heart is glad, and my glory rejoiceth. . . . " That is another way of saying that he found great joy in God. So here was David's pattern—to always live to the glory of God and consequently to enjoy God forever—the same statement as the catechism which came such a long time later.

Let me repeat it: the supreme objective in the life of any man or woman should be to give God glory. And the great consequence of that goal is unbounded joy. I believe that spiritual maturity may be summed up in the life which concentrates and focuses on the Person of God until one is caught up and lost in His majesty. A man does not fulfill his purpose Godward until he glorifies God, nor does he fulfill his purpose in the personal aspect until he experiences the fullness of joy.

Now, God is not an ogre. He is not sitting up there in heaven demanding that we glorify Him only for His own benefit. Rather, He promises that if we glorify Him, He will give us joy in return.

Definitions—*God's Intrinsic Glory.* What do we mean by glorifying God? We can look at it practically from two aspects. The first concerns the glory that God has in Himself. By that I mean that the glory of God is intrinsic to His very nature. Consider Isaiah 6:3, which records the words of the seraphim: "And one cried unto another, and said, Holy, holy, holy, is the Lord of hosts: the whole earth is full of his glory."

God possesses intrinsic glory by virtue of who He is. This is not given to Him. If man had never been created, if the angels had never been created, would God still be a God of glory? Certainly! If no one ever gave Him any glory, any honor, or any praise, would He still be the glorious God that He is? Of course! That is intrinsic glory—the glory of God's nature. It is the manifestation and combination of all His attributes. (This is clear from Exodus 33:18, 19).

This aspect of Gods glory is as essential to Him as light is to the sun, as blue is to the sky, as wet is to water. You don't have to command the sun to shine. It just does. You don't have to make water wet. It is. Nor do you need to paint the sky blue. That is its color already. So it is with the glory of God. We cannot give it to Him; we cannot diminish it. He *is* who He is. He is all of His attributes in perfect harmony—the "God of glory" (Acts 7:2).

"Well, what about Titus 2:10?" you ask—"Not purloining, but shewing all good fidelity; that they may adorn the doctrine of God our Saviour in all things." But this verse does *not* say that it is possible to adorn God. While we cannot adorn God, we can adorn the doctrine of God. In other words, by living a holy life, we adorn the doctrine of God, but not God. If we live the way we wish, it will not affect God, but it may affect the testimony about God in the world. Again, God has intrinsic glory that we cannot do anything about—we cannot add to it and we cannot take it away.

Now the glory of man is quite unlike that. A man's glory is granted to him. We talk about men being exalted and honored. But if you take off a king's robes and crown, strip him naked, and put him next to a beggar, you would not be able to tell which is which. The only glory a king enjoys is that bestowed upon him by fancy clothes and a handsome throne to sit on. But he has no intrinsic glory.

On the other hand, the glory of God resides in His essence, His nature. It is His being, as basic to Him as His grace, His mercy, His power, and His knowledge. Those constitute infinities. All we do is to recognize them. So we say, "Yes, it's true: God is glorious!"

In addition to various Old Testament reference (*see* Psalms 24:7–10), the New Testament supports this same concept. In relation to the Lord Jesus Christ, it is said that He was glory incarnate (John 1:14).

The raising of Lazarus illustrates the Saviour's glory. You recall how Jesus tarried beyond Jordan until He knew that Lazarus was dead. Jesus loved Lazarus deeply, but He waited for his death in order to perform a miracle. When the Lord ordered the removal of the gravestone, Martha protested. But Jesus answered, "Said I not unto thee, that, if thou wouldest believe, thou shouldest see the glory of God?" (John 11:40).

What was the glory of God in this instance? What attribute was about to be displayed? Power—the same mighty power that God used in Creation—was now about to be put on display in the raising of Lazarus. Martha did not *give* God this glory. It is something He already had. But here His nature was about to be revealed in glory. And it was.

In John 17:24 Jesus prayed, "Father, I will that they also, whom thou hast given me, be with me where I am; that they may behold my glory, which thou hast given me. . . . " The answer to that prayer will be realized in Revelation 21:23, which describes the New Jerusalem as having no need of sun or moon, " . . . for the glory of God did lighten it, and the Lamb is the light thereof." How beautifully this shows that glory is an essential, intrinsic part of God's very nature.

Since this is true, the glory of God is something which He does not give to man. Isaiah 48:11 tells us, " . . . and I will not give my glory unto another." God does not give away His nature.

Jesus plants His glory within us, but He never plants His glory upon us or within us apart from Himself. By saying that God gives His glory to the believer, we mean that He Himself comes to dwell in the believer. The glory never becomes the recipient's. God never divests Himself of His glory.

An illustration might be the ring which Pharaoh gave to Joseph. He took it off and gave it to Joseph and also put upon him a gold chain (Genesis 41:42). "Only in the throne will I be greater than thou," Pharaoh said (*see* v. 40)—"I'll give you a ring and I'll give you a chain, but I'll keep my throne." Even as this, God does not give up His glory.

So there we have the first aspect of our definition of God's glory. It is something intrinsic to Him that He possesses alone in Himself. It is the sum of His attributes. It cannot be diminished.

Enhancing God's Glory Before People. But there is a second aspect. Although we have pointed out that the glory of God cannot be added to, there is a sense in which the creatures of God may bring glory to Him. That is by magnifying God's glory before the world. This is not, however, adding to His nature, but merely enhancing God's glory before people.

An Old Testament book makes this very plain—First Chronicles. David says, "Declare his glory among the heathen; his marvellous works among all nations" (16:24). Note that the first word is "declare," not "give." Declaring glory is not the same as giving it: "Glory and honour are in his presence . . ." (v. 27). Again, this tells us of the intrinsic nature of God.

Another verse makes it even clearer. David says of God, "Thine, O Lord, is the greatness, and the power, and the glory, and the victory, and the majesty: for all that is in the heaven and in the earth is thine; thine is the kingdom, O Lord, and thou art exalted as head above all" (1 Chronicles 29:11). After making that declaration, David summed up. "Now therefore, our God, we thank thee, and praise thy glorious name" (v. 13). David merely recognized what was already true—that God possessed glory innately, and that He ought to be praised because of it.

Another example—from the New Testament: Paul prayed that "Christ shall be magnified in my body" (*see* Philippians 1:20). He didn't mean that he could improve upon Christ. He meant that he might exalt Christ in the eyes of the world. When we exalt God, when we praise Him, when we lift Him up, we glorify God. That is what the apostle meant when he said, ". . . glorify God in your body, and in your spirit, which are God's" (1 Corinthians 6:20). In other words, give pure testimony to the pure glory of God, that men might see it.

Paul gives another example in 1 Timothy 1:17: "Now unto

the King eternal, immortal, invisible, the only wise God, be
honour and glory for ever and ever. Amen." And at the end of
this book, Paul speaks of God as the One "Who only hath im-
mortality, dwelling in the light which no man can approach
unto; whom no man hath seen, nor can see: to whom be honour
and power everlasting. Amen" (1 Timothy 6:16). The apostle
is not saying that men can add to God's intrinsic glory but that
they can bring Him glory by allowing Him to be seen in them
by others.

The same is true in the little Book of Jude. "To the only wise
God our Saviour, be glory and majesty, dominion and power,
both now and ever. Amen" (Jude 25). And in Revelation we find
great hosts of people saying, "Glory, glory, glory." And so it is
that we magnify God before the world—but we do not add to
His nature.

Glory of God Past.   Now having dealt with those two aspects
of God's glory—the fact that it is intrinsic and that men may
declare it—let's look at this theme more fully as revealed in the
Bible. Biblical history reveals *the glory of God past.* Bible
prophecy foretells *the glory of God future.* And in the church
of our day, we see *the glory of God present.* As we consider
these various time periods, we discover that God's method in
revealing His glory is to take lowly things that have no glory
in themselves and transform them to be used as instruments to
show forth His glory and to bring Him praise.

Creation Shows It.   Whatever facet of God's activity that we
consider, we find that it was made for the purpose of the glory
of God and Christ. Look at Creation. "The heavens declare the
glory of God; and the firmament sheweth his handywork"
(Psalms 19:1). And who was the Creator? Colossians 1:16 gives
the answer: "For by him were all things created, that are in
heaven, and that are in earth, visible and invisible, whether
they be thrones, or dominions, or principalities, or powers: all
things were created by him, and for him." Creation was
brought into existence for the glory of God and Christ. The
universe and man were made that they might bear witness to

and reflect the glory of the all-glorious God. Their purpose is to praise God because He deserves it.

Now in all the universe of every single thing that God ever made, from the smallest microscopic life to the most vast unchartered ball of flame in the sky, only two things fail to give Him glory—fallen angels and fallen man. God is going to cast these two categories out of His presence eternally. Since the purpose of everything is to give God glory, that which doesn't is excused from existing in His presence. Even that removal reflects God's glory, in a sense, because it shows His righteousness against sin. So in a negative way it brings Him glory.

Now God is not happy to get glory in this fashion—by consigning the wicked to hell. The Bible assures us that God has no pleasure in the death of the wicked (Ezekiel 33:11). And hell was created for the devil and his angels (Matthew 25:41).

First in Eden. The glory of God is a continuous theme in Scripture. How is it that the Bible reveals the glory of God past? He did it first in the Garden of Eden where He personally manifested His glory to Adam and Eve. Genesis 3:8 tells us that this first pair heard the voice of the Lord walking in the Garden in the cool of the day. But this same verse also tells us that, in an effort to escape responsibility for their sin, they attempted to hide themselves from the presence of the Lord. So it is evident that God came to them not only through a voice but in some visible manifestation of His glory.

Now what was the nature of that presence? Evidence suggests that God's glorious attributes were transformed as a brilliant shining light. Hebrew has a word for it—*shekinah*, meaning to dwell or to reside with. It was used by Jews and later by Christians to express the visible divine presence of God.

So right at the beginning of human history, God manifested Himself to Adam and Eve in order that they might recognize Him as the glorious God and pay Him the glory He was due. What a fantastic privilege Adam and Eve enjoyed—this daily viewing of God's glory! How long they continued to enjoy that sight, no one knows. But the day came when they decided to usurp a little authority themselves and to be wise and to know right from wrong. In that act they became unfit to share His presence—to even be in the same place where His glory was. So God cast them out. He punctuated His expulsion by stationing cherubim at the east of the Garden. This was an order of created being usually associated with guarding the holiness of God. A flaming sword turned every way to cut off access to the tree of life (Genesis 3:24). This same principle holds true today—fallen men are dismissed from God's presence just as were the fallen angels. Either we give glory to God or we are not allowed in His presence.

Adam and Eve finished out their lives with that sword blocking any hope of reentering the Garden. It cut them off from having their previous communion with God. The sword spoke of judgment. That sword had to fall on something before the human race could ever again have communion with God. On whom did the sword fall? On our Saviour Jesus. "For Christ also hath once suffered for sins, the just for the unjust, that he might bring us to God. . . " (1 Peter 3:18). The only way to regain fellowship with God is through allowing Christ to bear the judgment. That happened at the cross.

More in Moses.   So we see that the glory of God was a part of Eden, but it was withdrawn from the rebellious and the proud. It next showed up in the life of one who was obedient and humble—in Moses, the man who did not believe he was good for anything. When God called this man to be His prophet and to lead His people, Moses begged off; remember? "Lord, I can't do it. I have a speech impediment" (*see* Exodus 4:10).

You can almost hear the Lord's response. "Oh, come now, Moses, who made your mouth?" But Moses still threw up objections until the Lord assigned Aaron to be his spokesman. What a nuisance! Yet God wanted to use Moses to reveal His glory to Israel, and when God's glory got inside this man, something really happened to him.

Let's pick up the story in Exodus 33. By this time Moses had assumed his role of leader of God's people. The law had been given. But the hard, difficult journey to the Promised Land lay before them. Moses reminds the Lord of his commission to bring the people out of captivity and to lead them forth. But now he prays, "If I have found grace in thy sight, show me now thy way, that I may know thee" (*see* v. 13). Moses knows he can't make it on his own. God assures Moses that His presence will go with him (v. 14).

But Moses still doubts his assignment from the Lord. So he asks for a miracle: "Show me thy glory" (*see* v. 18). Would God do it? How Moses must have strained to hear the reply. "I will make all my goodness pass before thee, and I will proclaim the name of the Lord before thee . . . " (v. 19).

The word *goodness* here refers to the manifestation or essence of God's glorious attributes, characterized by grace and mercy. Now that is dangerous to look at! Stare at the sun with your eyes unprotected and you will go blind. Get too close and you will go up in smoke. The sun is devastating in its brilliance. And since the Creator is always greater than the Creation, what must it be like to look at God? To stare unprotected at His glory would have meant instant death—complete consummation. God is a flaming fire.

So God says, "Moses, I can't let you see My face or you'll die. No man can do that and live. But go stand in that space in the rock. I'll cover you with My hands and then I'll open My fingers just a little bit so you can look through and see My glory go by" (*see* Exodus 33:21–23).

Does God have a face? A hand? No, God is a spirit without physical form. Yet He often uses words referring to the body in order to allow us to understand in some measure what He is like. So when God speaks of His face or hand, He is accommodating Himself to our terms.

"And the Lord descended in the cloud, and stood with him there, and proclaimed the name of the Lord. And the Lord passed by before him, and proclaimed, The Lord, The Lord God, merciful and gracious, longsuffering, and abundant in goodness and truth, Keeping mercy for thousands, forgiving iniquity and transgression and sin. . . " (Exodus 34:5–7). All Moses could do was to make haste, bow his head toward the earth, and glorify God (v. 8).

Reflected Glory and the Veil.   What was the effect of the
shekinah glory upon Moses? A little bit of God's afterglow
rubbed off on him and his face beamed with the glory of God.
His face was literally charged with the glory of God—but all
unknown to Moses. In fact, his face shone so much that Aaron
and the others feared to approach him (vv. 29, 30). Imagine—
the glory of God reflected on the face of a man!

When I was a little kid, my folks took me one time to Knott's
Berry Farm, which had a store over by the lake which sold all
kinds of items which glowed in the dark. I thought it was the
greatest thing I had ever seen. "Why don't you pick out one
you like and we'll take it home," my parents suggested. So I
selected a little figure. I kept it in a bag all day. Home at last,
when darkness had fallen I took it out and placed it upon my
dresser. Nothing happened. It didn't glow and I was really up-
set.

"Do you know why it doesn't glow?" my father asked. "You
see, you have to hold it up to some other light because it doesn't
have any of its own." So my dad held it up next to a light bulb
for a minute or so and then I took it back to my darkened room.
Boy! This time it worked!

Do you see the similarity between that little figure and
Moses? He had no light of his own, either. But after standing
near the most brilliant light in the universe, he glowed. His face
was charged with the glory of God. The Lord chose to send
Moses off that mountaintop with a little of the glow of deity.
For a time Moses placed a veil over his face so that the people
could come near him. Only when Moses reentered the presence of God did he remove the veil. Then he would speak to
the Lord in open fellowship. The glory on Moses' face would
be briefly renewed, and again required him to veil his face
when talking with the people (vv. 33–35).

But there is another reason for his wearing of the veil—one
not so immediately evident. Let me refer again to my illustration. Do you know what happened to that little figure I had
sitting on top of my dresser? After an hour or so, it did not glow
anymore. It became dark because the light was not its own. And

this is what Moses experienced. Moses veiled himself because the glory was gradually fading away, and he didn't want the people to see him lose the radiance.

We can be sure of that because the New Testament tells us that Moses put a veil over his face " . . . that the children of Israel could not stedfastly look to the end of that which is abolished" (2 Corinthians 3:13). Moses knew that the glory was not his own, that it was fading, and he didn't want his people to see the glory leave his face.

Twice in human history God had shown His glory—once in a place, once in a face. The people of Israel must have wondered if ever again in their lifetime they would see the glory of God.

Glory in a Tent.   They did—in a place called the Tabernacle, which was built to glorify God. Earlier I pointed out that God deigns to use lowly, humble things to reveal His glory. And He continued that pattern in what He chose to do in the Tabernacle. We often think of it as a pretty place, but it possessed no exterior beauty, since it consisted of many weather-beaten, dull, unattractive animal skins. It was just an ugly tent. Yet God would use even that to show His glory.

God gave detailed instructions as to how the Tabernacle was to be constructed. When at last it was finished, "Then a cloud covered the tent of the congregation, and the glory of the Lord filled the tabernacle. And Moses was not able to enter into the tent of the congregation, because the cloud abode thereon, and the glory of the Lord filled the tabernacle" (Exodus 40:34, 35). Picture the scene: the twelve tribes of Israel—perhaps several million people—each lined up in order, as God has positioned them. Right in the middle was the Tabernacle and in the center of that, the glory of God filling the place so much so that no one could get in!

Later, on the Day of Atonement, the high priest would walk into the holy of holies and step up to the Ark. Now many people think that was a gorgeous article of furniture, but it was probably plain and encrusted with the sacrificial blood that had been sprinkled on it. The only beautiful thing about it would have

been the wings of the cherubim stretched out over the mercy
seat. And what was there? The *shekinah* glory—the glory of
God. Each time the high priest entered into that sacred place,
he saw the glory of God.

Next in the Temple.   For several hundred years the Tabernacle served as the manifestation point of God's glory, but as
in the Garden and on the face of Moses, this glory was only
temporary. One day the tent was taken down and stored away
to be replaced by a magnificent building. Just as God had given
instructions concerning the building of the Tabernacle, so He
gave blueprints for the building of the Temple. Its purpose was
to house the glory of God. Some Bible scholars estimate that the
elaborate and beautiful building cost up to fifteen million dol-
lars. Construction went forward for almost eight years until at
last it was finished.

And what a day of dedication! "And it came to pass, when
the priests were come out of the holy place, that the cloud filled
the house of the Lord, So that the priests could not stand to
minister because of the cloud: for the glory of the Lord had
filled the house of the Lord" (1 Kings 8:10, 11). Once again, God
in His condescending grace had moved right down with His
presence into the lives of His people.

But it wasn't permanent this time either, because although
the Temple was built for the glory of God, He didn't always
receive it. On one occasion Solomon did. Second Chronicles
relates the story of the state visit of the Queen of Sheba to King
Solomon's court. When she had tested his wisdom, surveyed all
his wealth, and viewed the Temple he had built, she flipped!
"There was no more spirit in her" (*see* 9:4). "They hadn't told
me the half of it," she gasped, and then she launched into her
own version of how wonderful Solomon was, how wise, how
lucky his servants were, what great things he had done, including, no doubt, what a marvelous Temple he had built. And she
left for home without ever realizing that it was God's glory that
dwelt in the Temple, not Solomon's. Unfortunately, the record
doesn't reveal that Solomon ever corrected her. And from that
point on, we see a great but gradual decline of the Temple.

When the Temple degenerated, you know what God had to do? The glorious God departed. He just removed His glory. Idolatry slowly moved in on God's glory. Temple worship had all but disappeared by the time the Prophet Ezekiel came along.

From Glory to Shame.   Ezekiel saw this in a vision. He entered the Temple, and what he saw just shattered his heart. He knew that the glory of God resided within the holy of holies, but outside he saw the worship of false gods being carried on. "So I went in and saw; and behold every form of creeping things, and abominable beasts, and all the idols of the house of Israel, pourtrayed upon the wall round about" (Ezekiel 8:10). Then he went into the inner court of the Lord's House and there he saw men with their backs toward the Temple of the Lord, bowed down with their faces toward the east, worshiping the sun (v. 16).

No wonder Ezekiel was so disturbed. God wasn't being worshiped and glorified in the Temple—Satan was. Let's get one thing straight: God is choosy about His company. When Satan comes in, God goes out.

The withdrawal of God's glory occurred in progressive stages, almost as if God reluctantly left in great sadness. Ezekiel recounts how the glory retreated step by step. The glory rose up from the sculptured cherub and stood over the doorway. Next, the glory departed from the doorway and rested on the wings of the living cherubims of Ezekiel's vision. Then the glory of God went up from the middle of Jerusalem and stood upon the mountain to the east. And finally the manifestation of glory was no longer visible, for it returned to heaven. God removed His glory from the Temple back to His throne.

Now, instead of glory shining above their heads, God again invoked the word *Ichabod*—"the glory has departed" (*see* 1 Samuel 4:21). The day came when even the magnificent Temple was no longer a fit receptacle for God's glory. No wonder God allowed the Babylonians to burn the building down. God's glory—gone! Would it ever come back?

Glory Incarnate.   Yes, God's glory did come back, but only after a very long time. Want to know when? Look at John 1:14.

I love this verse. It gives me goose bumps. "And the Word was made flesh, and dwelt among us, (and we beheld his glory, the glory as of the only begotten of the Father,) full of grace and truth."

God's glory came back in the Person of our Lord Jesus Christ. When was it most fully manifested? On the mountaintop at the time of the Transfiguration (Luke 9:28–36). There, for a few minutes in the presence of three disciples, the Son of God allowed all His splendor to shine through. Here was glory—not as a glow in the Garden, nor as a reflection on Moses' face, nor in the brightness of the Tabernacle or Temple, but glory intrinsic to the God-Man—Jesus Christ.

Although the glory of Christ is permanent like His other attributes, this manifestation of it was only temporary. One day wicked men condemned Him falsely, nailed Him to a tree, and removed Him out of their sight. They extinguished the greatest expression of the glory of God.

Glory to Come.   Will it ever appear again? Our Lord personally gave the answer when He talked one day with His disciples. How exciting just to read of it. He told them of a period of great tribulation which would one day fall upon this world. At the end of this time—a spectacular happening: "And then shall appear the sign of the Son of man in heaven: and then shall all the tribes of the earth mourn, and they shall see the Son of man coming in the clouds of heaven with power and great glory" (Matthew 24:30).

Now what is the sign Jesus speaks of? I believe it is the unmatched manifestation of His glory—the *shekinah* glory—which God revealed at the times and places and occasions we have been looking at. It is the total brilliance of God coming down out of heaven in the Person of our Lord.

Once again, sinful men will try to extinguish it. They will oppose Him, even though He comes as *"KING OF KINGS, AND LORD OF LORDS"* (*see* Revelation 19:16). When they see His flaming glory descending out of the sky, they will fire off their missiles, hoping to blow that glory out of the sky. But they won't be able to do it. With only a word, Jesus will exterminate those who seek to restrain His glory. From that time on, He will rule the nations with a rod of iron and will reign on David's throne with power and glory—far greater glory than He revealed at His first advent.

Do you want to know something exciting? *We're going to be there.* All the dead in Christ, as well as those caught up to be with Him at the Rapture, will return with Him at this moment. That is fantastic, but absolutely true. The Word of God promises it: "When Christ, who is our life, shall appear, then shall ye also appear with him in glory" (Colossians 3:4). When He comes back, He will give us new glorified bodies fit to enjoy His glorious presence forever.

"What are we going to do then?" you may wonder. Give Him glory. In the last book of the Bible we learn of a tremendous group which appears before His throne. John writes, "After this I beheld, and, lo, a great multitude, which no man could number, of all nations, and kindreds, and people, and tongues, stood before the throne, and before the Lamb, clothed with white robes, and palms in their hands; And cried with a loud voice, saying, Salvation to our God which sitteth upon the throne, and unto the Lamb" (Revelation 7:9, 10).

And as if that were not enough, John tells us of a further chorus: "Saying, Amen: Blessing, and glory, and wisdom, and thanksgiving, and honour, and power, and might, be unto our God for ever and ever. Amen" (v. 12).

Glory, glory, glory—that's the point of everything—that God receives the glory due Him from all of His Creation. And we are going to behold that glory all through eternity. Imagine, if you can, ". . . that great city, the holy Jerusalem, descending out of heaven from God, Having the glory of God . . ." (Revelation 21:10, 11). "And the city had no need of the sun, neither of the moon, to shine in it: for the glory of God did lighten it, and the Lamb is the light thereof" (v. 23).

Glory in the Present.   We have taken a brief look at the glory of God past, as revealed in the Old Testament period and in the time of our Lord's earthly ministry. We have also caught a glimpse of the glory that shall be. Now, what about the glory of God present? Where is the glory now?

Right here—in the body of Christ. It is our privilege, our purpose, our duty to manifest the glory of God. Paul tells us that we are a holy temple housing the glory of God (Ephesians 2:21, 22). One of the purposes of His body, the church, is "to give the light of the knowledge of the glory of God in the face of Jesus Christ" (*see* 2 Corinthians 4:6). Although we are earthen vessels—clay pots, if you will—we carry about the glory of God.

I like that. God has chosen the humble things, the absolute "nothing" things to bring glory to Himself. He transforms us by the power of the Holy Spirit and allows us to radiate glory. Now since this is true, we had better be shining. If the world is ever going to get the message of the glory, it must come through us. People must see Christ in us, the hope of glory (Colossians 1:27). The more mature we are, the more we can be used to radiate God's glory. "Whether therefore ye eat, or drink, or whatsoever ye do, do all to the glory of God" (1 Corinthians 10:31).

Glory for His Name.   Now some Christians witness for the Lord out of a sense of obedience because they are commanded to do so. They want to share the Gospel because of their love and concern for the lost. That is a worthy motive, but not the highest one.

The supreme motive for evangelism should be the glory of God. That is what moved the Apostle Paul. He labored, he preached, he poured out his heart "for his name" (Romans 1:5). Yes, he loved the lost. Yes, he reached them at the command of Christ. But Paul passionately desired to bring others to the Saviour in order to give Him glory. He considered it a tremendous injustice for anybody to go out into eternity and not give God glory. If God is God and God alone and the sole Creator and the Lord of men, then He has a right to exclusive worship and a right to be jealous if He is not worshiped.

Henry Martyn, that godly missionary to India, watched people bowing down before their idols. "Seeing these people prostrate before Hindu gods excited more horror in me than I can express. . . . I could not endure existence if Jesus was not glorified. It would be hell to me."

I must confess that God has rebuked me time and again because I don't always feel that way. It just isn't "hell to me" to see somebody who does not glorify Jesus Christ. But I pray that God will give me such a love for the glory of Jesus that it will drive a stake through my heart every time someone rejects Him—every time someone doesn't give Him the glory He deserves.

And why not? "Wherefore God also hath highly exalted him, and given him a name which is above every name: That at the name of Jesus every knee should bow . . . And that every tongue should confess that Jesus Christ is Lord, to the glory of God the Father" (Philippians 2:9–11). The hymnist was right when he wrote, "Let ev'ry kindred, ev'ry tribe, On this terrestrial ball, To Him all majesty ascribe, And crown Him Lord of all."

The glory of God—we see it in the heavens, in the earth, in salvation, in Christian living, in the promised return of Christ, in every dimension that God deals with. I call it the Master Purpose for unlocking all the spiritual riches hidden in Jesus Christ. Now, if this is the Master Purpose, the frame for living, how can you build upon it? How can you glorify God? For that, you need something more—the Master Plan.

2

The Master Plan—
How to Glorify God

The supreme thing in the life of a man or woman—in the life of anybody who has ever been born into this world—is to glorify God. That is what living is all about. It is the end result of the Christian life. Spiritual maturity is simply concentrating and focusing on the Person of God until we are caught up in His majesty and His glory.

Why Glorify God?   Let's look briefly at the *why* before we get to the *how*. The most obvious reason to glorify God stems from the fact that He created us. Psalm 100 states it simply: "It is he that hath made us" (*see* v. 3). Compare that with Romans 11:36: "For of him, and through him, and to him, are all things: to whom be glory for ever. Amen." Why does God deserve glory? Because He gave us our being, our life, and everything that is—that is reason number one.

Second, we ought to glorify God because He made everything to give Him glory. Proverbs 16:4 says, "The Lord hath made all things for himself. . . ." He made everything to speak His glory, everything to radiate His glory—everything. Creation shows His attributes, His power, His love, His mercy, His wisdom, His grace. And all Creation gives Him glory. The stars do—"The heavens declare the glory of God . . ." (Psalms 19:1). Animals do—"The beast of the field shall honour me . . ." (Isaiah 43:20). The angels give Him glory. At the birth of Christ they said, "Glory to God in the highest . . . " (Luke 2:14). If these things which are lower in the rank of Creation than man glorify God, can we do less than give Him the glory due His name?

God even gets glory out of unbelievers who do not choose to glorify Him. Chalk it up as reason number three—the fact that God judges those who refuse to glorify Him. A good example is Pharaoh sitting on the throne of Egypt at the time God released His children from bondage. This man fought against God for all he was worth. But God declared, "I will get me honour from Pharaoh" (*see* Exodus 14:17). And He did. He got it. Sooner or later, everyone will give God glory, willingly or unwillingly.

How to Glorify God.   I would like to suggest thirteen practical ways to glorify God, not in any particular order of importance.

Glory Through Salvation.   The first way—receive the Lord Jesus Christ as your Saviour. That's basic. You cannot begin to give God glory until you come to Christ. Up to that point, you haven't acknowledged God. To come to Christ is to give Him glory. "Wherefore God also hath highly exalted him [Christ], and given him a name which is above every name [Christ is greater than any other]: That at the name of Jesus every knee should bow, of things in heaven, and things in earth, and things under the earth; And that every tongue should confess that Jesus Christ is Lord, to the glory of God the Father" (Philippians 2:9–11). God is glorified when we bow and confess Jesus as Lord. If you want to give God glory, begin here.

On Target.   Point two—glorify God by aiming your life at that high purpose. That is the beginning of everything. You will never glorify God in your life until you aim in that direction. The command in 1 Corinthians 10:31 takes in a great deal of territory: "Whether therefore ye eat, or drink, or whatsoever ye do, do all to the glory of God." Even such mundane things as eating and drinking ought to be done to His glory. That is what is meant by aiming at His glory. Our Lord said, "And I seek not mine own glory [but the glory of him that sent me]" (John 8:50). In other words: "I live to bring Him glory, I live

to radiate His attributes. I live to adorn the doctrine of God.
I live to exalt God in the eyes of the world. This is the purpose
of my life."

Now the first principle of aiming for the glory of God is to
sacrifice self and self-glory. Hypocrites come along and try to
steal the glory of God. "I want a little glory for myself," they
think. Remember those that Jesus warned about in Matthew 6—the alms givers? "When you do your alms," Jesus said,
"don't sound a trumpet." Can you imagine that? This fellow
carries along a few trumpeters to play a little fanfare as he
arrives at the Temple to drop his coins in the box. "Here I am,
folks. See me?" Plunk, plunk. The Lord said they did this, "that
they may have glory" (*see* v. 2). God does not reward the kind
of giving that competes for His glory.

Even born-again Christians have to beware of trying to steal
glory from God. A young man once came up to D. L. Moody
and said, "Mr. Moody, we've just been to an all-night prayer
meeting. See how our faces shine!" Moody replied, "Moses
knew not that his face shone." Straight stuff! Don't try to take
any glory from God. You are the loser, and you can't get it
anyway.

Another way to aim your life to the glory of God is to *prefer
Him above all else.* We place Him above all things—money,
fame, honor, success, friends, even family. I can think of times
when I have gone to speak somewhere, and in the back of my
mind I am saying to myself, "I hope they like me. My, I bet they
really like me." That is disgusting. If what I say is not for the
glory of God—but for myself—I might as well shut my mouth.
If I teach a Bible study for my own glory, God's blessing is not
on that. I must prefer His glory above everything else.

In preferring God above all else, you may have to pay a price.
In Exodus 32 some people paid a very dear price. The occasion
was the orgy and idolatry of the people at the foot of the mountain where Moses was receiving the Ten Commandments.
When Moses came down and saw it, he said, "Who is on the
Lord's side? Let him come to me" All the sons of Levi, the
priests, moved. Then Moses said, "Put every man his sword by

his side and go in and out from gate to gate through the camp. Slay every man his brother, his companion, and his neighbor." Would they carry out that order? They did, and 3,000 fell (*see* vv. 26–28). You see, the glory of God was at stake. And God shares His glory with no other. These people had to pay the price of actually killing those they loved—for the sake of the glory of God.

Another aspect of aiming at God's glory is that *we do it when we are content to do His will at any cost.* Jesus prayed, "Now is my soul troubled; and what shall I say? Father, save me from this hour: but for this cause came I unto this hour. Father, glorify thy name . . ." (John 12:27, 28). And in the Garden of Gethsemane, Jesus prayed, "Father, let this cup pass from me; nevertheless, not my will but thine be done" (*see* Matthew 26:39, 42; Mark 14:36; Luke 22:42). In other words, "Father, if You are going to get glory out of this, I submit to it. Glorify Thy name, Father, whatever it costs Me."

Aiming at God's glory also means that *you suffer when He suffers*—that you hurt when God's name is hurt. Remember Psalms 69:9: "For the zeal of thine house hath eaten me up; and the reproaches of them that reproached thee are fallen upon me." David was saying, "I hurt when God hurts."

I was sitting in my office thinking over this point—just asking myself if I really aim at God's glory to the extent that I hurt inside when God's name is defamed. Then a letter came in from a seventeen-year-old girl whom my sister had the privilege of leading to Christ. The problems in her background were just unbelievable. After receiving Christ, she had to return to her home in a distant city with no Christian friends, no spiritual instruction, with nothing except her Bible and people praying for her. Several months later she wrote:

> I hope everything is well with you. I have really begun to put things together in the Bible. By reading the Old Testament I have been able to see that God deserves much more recognition than He's getting. I can see how He gave people so many chances and how they continued to break His heart

by worshipping idols and sinning. God wanted the Israelites to sacrifice lambs, goats, oxen and things like that as an atonement to Him for sin. He is God, after all, and He had to have some payment for the trouble and the sins of men.

To think that God actually talked and was in the visible presence of these people and yet they kept on complaining and sinning! I can almost feel the unbearable sadness that God feels when someone rejects and doesn't glorify Him. He's God! He made us. He gave us everything. We continue to doubt and reject Him. It's awful! When I think of how I hurt Him, I hope I can someday make it up.

I have a soft spot in my heart for God. I can feel His jealousy now when I see people worshipping idols and other gods. It's all so clear to me that God must be glorified. He deserves it, and it's long overdue.

I can't wait to just tell Jesus, and thus God indirectly, that I love Him and just kiss the ground He walks on because He should be worshipped. I want God to be God and to take His rightful place. I'm tired of the way people put Him down.

All by herself, with her Bible and the Holy Spirit, this young girl came to realize that the glory of God was what life was all about. I know some people who have been Christians for decades and haven't learned this truth. That is the purpose of our existence—to give God glory, and part of that means hurting when He hurts.

Another angle on this: aiming at God's glory also involves *being content to be outdone by others in gifts and honors just so God gets the glory.* We aim at His glory when we willingly take a backseat and see somebody else lifted up—somebody else honored—just as long as God gets the glory.

The life of Paul gives us an excellent illustration. His great goal was to exalt God through Jesus Christ. He did that actively until the time came when he was shut up in prison. Had that happened to us, we might have considered ourselves to have been shelved. But Paul took it in his stride because he was trusting God that even this would be a means of glorifying Him. And it was.

But meanwhile, those on the outside were seeking to hurt Paul mentally and emotionally. "[They] preach Christ of contention, not sincerely, supposing to add affliction to my bonds," he wrote (Philippians 1:16). That could have been painful for Paul. While he was confined in that rotten prison, others were free on the outside—free to preach, free to teach, free to win the love of those brought to Christ.

So what was Paul's reaction? "What then? notwithstanding, every way, whether in pretence, or in truth, Christ is preached; and I therein do rejoice, yea, and will rejoice" (v. 18). The apostle didn't care who got the credit, as long as the Lord was glorified.

How about you? What are your inner feelings when someone who does what you do gains greater honor? How do you react? One mark of spiritual maturity is being willing to let others have the credit. The thermometer of your Christian life will register whether you are concerned with His glory or with your own.

Admit It.   A third way we give God glory is by the confession of sin. Perhaps you hadn't thought of it, but when you confess sin, you really glorify God.

A good illustration comes from the Book of Joshua and the story of Achan (Joshua 7). You remember how, in direct violation of God's orders, this man gathered up part of the spoils after the fall of Jericho. "Nobody will know; nobody will find out," he thought as he buried them in a hole under his tent. "God will never know. He can't see through the dirt." But God did know, and Achan was found out. And what did Joshua say? "My son, give, I pray thee, glory to the Lord God of Israel , and make confession unto him . . ." (v. 19).

Confession of sin glorifies God, because if you excuse your sin, you impune God. You say that you are helpless and that God lets you get into a mess. Adam illustrates this. When God pinned him to the wall, what was his excuse? "The woman whom thou gavest to be with me . . ." (Genesis 3:12)—"You did it, God. If You hadn't given me this woman, this never would have happened."

To do this is assigning to God the possibility of unrighteousness. But God is not at fault. He is never at fault. God never in any way acts unrighteously, and whenever an individual tries to sneak out from under the absolute responsibility for his own sin, he impunes the character of God.

A helpful illustration comes from 1 Samuel. The children of Israel had not paid any attention to God for years until they got into a big battle with the Philistines. Someone said, "We're in trouble! We've got to get God up here. Go down and get the Ark." The Ark represented God. When it arrived on the front line, the Israelites jumped up and down. "Hurray! Hurray! The Ark is here—the day is won!" (*see* 4: 2–5). But the Philistines captured the Ark and stuck it in the temple of Dagon, their false god. God did not like that place, so He began chopping away at the idol (5:1–4).

And God was not through. "But the hand of the Lord was heavy upon them of Ashdod, and he destroyed them, and smote them with emerods . . ." (5:6). All the men of the city developed emerods in their secret parts (v. 9). The word *emerods* has been translated variously as hemorrhoids or tumors. God was smiting them for their mistreatment of the Ark.

Now their response was most interesting. They cried out to heaven, to God (v. 12). Chapter 6 recounts that they decided to return the Ark and to appease God by making a trespass offering. Apparently a plague of mice had struck the Philistines at the same time, so following their pagan custom, they made a votive offering which included likenesses of the diseased parts. They made golden images of the emerods and mice in order to "give glory unto the God of Israel" (*see* v. 5).

This act gave glory to God because it constituted a confession of sin. It was an acknowledgment that the evil which befell them resulted from their offense of God. And once they came and made their offerings and confession, they "exonerated" God and exalted His holy reaction against their evil. They said, in effect, "God, You had a right to act as You did because of what we did." That gave God glory.

When chastisement comes into your life in the sense of discipline from God, react by saying, "God, I deserve every bit of it! I know that because You are holy, You had to do what You did." That gives God glory.

We will get to the subject of confession in chapter 5. But let me point out right here that the Greek word for confession is *homologeō,* meaning "to say the same thing." We don't have to beg God for forgiveness. To confess means to agree with God that sin is all our fault, and to repent. This act glorifies God.

Glorify Through Faith.   A fourth way to glorify God is to trust Him. Romans 4:20 says that Abraham was "strong in faith, giving glory to God." God is glorified when you trust Him. Unbelief questions God and detracts from His glory.

The greatest problem about getting God's glory to the world is that it has to go through us! We like to quote the verse: "But my God shall supply all your need, according to his riches in glory by Christ Jesus" (Philippians 4:19). But then some crisis comes into our lives and we are wiped out. We collapse—and everybody at the job and at home knows it. And people say, "Some kind of God you've got! You don't even trust Him yourself." You see, God is glorified when we believe in Him, when we rest in His full assurance. That gives Him glory.

In this connection I always think of the three Hebrew children and their experience in the fiery furnace. When about to be thrown in, they didn't say, "We've got a practical problem. What verse applies here?" No, they made a flat announcement: "The God whom we serve is able to deliver us, and will deliver us" (*see* Daniel 3:17). With that, they walked in. If they had panicked, fallen to the ground, and groveled in the dirt before the golden image, that would not have glorified God.

God is glorified when we trust Him! If I were to ask you, "Do you think God keeps His word?" you would probably say *yes*. And then if I asked you if you live as if God keeps His word, you would say, "Well, I . . . . " That's one reason why the world isn't too sure of what kind of God we have. Let's glorify God by trusting Him. Not to trust Him is to make Him a liar (1 John 5:10).

Always in Season   Number five—we glorify God by fruitfulness. Remember John 15:8? "In this is my Father glorified, that

ye bear much fruit. . . ." Why? Because then the world can see
the results of a God-filled life—like the people who looked at
Israel of old and said, "Who is a god like unto their God who
does these wonders?" (*See* Deuteronomy 4:7.)

The Bible echoes this thought repeatedly. "Being filled with
the fruits of righteousness, which are by Jesus Christ, unto the
glory and praise of God" (Philippians 1:11). God planted us. He
expects fruit. His character is at stake in the eyes of men by the
fruitfulness of the life of the Christian. "But ye are a chosen
generation, a royal priesthood, an holy nation, a peculiar people; that ye should shew forth the praises of him who hath called
you out of darkness into his marvellous light" (1 Peter 2:9). That
is what we are here for—to put God on display to the world.

Colossians 1:10 takes us a step further: "That ye might walk
worthy of the Lord unto all pleasing, being fruitful in every
good work. . . ." Fruit is good works. When we live a life of
good works, the world will see and glorify our Father in heaven.

With a Capital P.   Ready for the sixth way to glorify God?
Praise Him! Psalms 50:23 says, "Whoso offereth praise glorifieth
me. . . ." Praise honors God. One way to offer praise is to recite
God's wonderful works. Sometimes, for example, a new Christian will come to me and ask if there is any reason to study the
Old Testament. I always give an emphatic *yes.* God wrote it,
and anything that God wrote I want to read. I can remember
that when I was courting my wife, she used to write me little
notes. I loved them and read them over again and again. When
you love someone, you are interested in what that one has to
say. The same is true of the Old Testament. I love God; therefore, I want to read what He wrote.

One reason that I ought to study the Old Testament is to
know the history of what God has done, so that I can recite it
to others. We can say, "God did this and this and this—how
wonderful are His works!" The record of the past is a continual
reminder that He has never proved unfaithful in history. What
did the disciples speak of on the day of Pentecost in languages
they had never learned? ". . . the wonderful works of God"
(Acts 2:11). The Jews traditionally exalted God for His wondrous

works, and so this outburst of praise caught their attention.

Another way to praise God is to give Him credit for everything. Remember how Joab fought against Rabbah and won the victory? When he got possession of the enemy crown, he sent for David that he might present the crown to him (2 Samuel 12:26–31). I've often thought that is a good illustration of how the Christian acts—or should. You win a victory in your life, but you don't wear the crown. You give it to the Lord who has gotten you the victory.

This Way, Too.   Let me suggest a seventh way by which to glorify God—suffer for Him. The Prophet Isaiah said to the remnant suffering persecution, "Glorify the Lord in the fires" (*see* Isaiah 24:15). Many have done just that. Micah languished in prison, Isaiah was sawn asunder, Paul was beheaded, and Luke, according to tradition, was hanged on an olive tree. But like those mentioned in Revelation 12:11, ". . . they loved not their lives unto the death."

Our Lord told Peter that he would die by crucifixion in order to glorify God (John 21:18,19). Peter underscored that concept when he wrote, "If ye be reproached for the name of Christ, happy are ye; for the spirit of glory and of God resteth upon you: on their part he is evil spoken of, but on your part he is glorified. . . . Yet if any man suffer as a Christian, let him not be ashamed; but let him glorify God on this behalf" (1 Peter 4:14, 16). When you suffer for Christ's sake, when you stand in front of this world and speak the truth and take the abuse, when you confront the system with the claims of Jesus Christ in boldness and courage, you glorify God. What a tremendous thing to be called to suffer for His sake!

Content With His Choice.   Number eight—glorify God by contentment. Discontent characterizes the age in which we live. We may be discontent about ourselves and about our circumstances. But who made you the way you are, minus your sins? God. So you ought to be content with yourself. Who put you in your present situation with all its circumstances, apart from sin? God did. You are what you are, whatever you are, wherever you are, because God put you there. When you are content, you acknowledge God's sovereignty in your life, and that gives Him glory. If you are discontent or malcontent, your real complaint is against God's wisdom.

"Now, MacArthur, don't tell me that God wanted me married to this woman!" you object. Well, maybe that was not God's primary objective—maybe your own will had a little to do with it. But once you married her, God wants that union to be all that it should be. And in His power, He can make it that.

I wish we had space to illustrate this extensively from the life of Paul. He testified, ". . . I have learned, in whatsoever state I am, therewith to be content. I know both how to be abased, and I know how to abound: every where and in all things I am instructed both to be full and to be hungry, both to abound and to suffer need" (Philippians 4:11, 12). This is the same man who catalogued his suffering in 2 Corinthians 11—his beatings, his imprisonments, his stoning, his shipwrecks, his perils, his weariness and pain, his hunger and thirst, his cold and nakedness.

Do you think you could give God glory in all that? Paul did. He said, "If I must needs glory, I will glory of the things which concern mine infirmities" (v. 30). He didn't say, "I'll give God glory in spite of my pain." He said, "I will give God glory *because* of it." Now that's a contented man.

Let me emphasize it again—discontent is a sin because it robs God of glory. A discontented Christian, for whatever reason—home, job, location, husband or wife, kids—is a terrible advertisement for the sovereignty of God. What kind of God do we have? Can He really be trusted? Can we be content in the circumstances in which He has placed us?

David said, "The Lord is the portion of mine inheritance. . ." (Psalms 16:5). And he added, "The lines are fallen unto me in pleasant places. . ." (v. 6). David was saying, "Since the Lord is the portion of my inheritance, since it is the Lord that I have received, the boundaries He gives me in life are pleasant."—". . . yea," he says, "I have a goodly heritage. I will bless the Lord . . ." (vv. 6, 7).

Glorifying God means that we praise Him with a full heart

in absolute contentment, knowing that our lot is God's plan for us now. Accepting it with contentment gives Him glory.

Glory Through Prayer. Number nine on our list—we give God glory by prayer. Jesus said, "And whatsoever ye shall ask in my name, that will I do. . ." (John 14:13). What a promise! If I were not a Christian and somebody told me that verse, that might be enough to convince me to become a believer—just to know that there was a God available to supply everything I asked.

But there is one qualification. Go back to the verse: "And whatsoever ye shall ask *in my name.*" We'll go into the meaning of this at length in chapter 7 on prayer. But let me say here that the qualification is not just a little zapper that we stick on the end of our prayers to get the things we want. Praying in Jesus' name is asking God in behalf of all that Jesus is—and all that He wills. As best I know Christ and understand His will, I ask because I feel this is what Jesus would want.

Jesus promised that He would answer, ". . . . that the Father may be glorified in the Son" (John 14:13). Prayer is for the glory of God. Have you ever had anybody stand up in a testimony meeting and say, "Such and such a thing was taking place, and we prayed about it, and God answered our prayer." And everybody says, "Praise the Lord!" That's the point. When you pray and God displays His power, He gets the glory. "Father, there's a sick person here. Heal him that Your glory may be known." That's how to pray. Not—"Heal that person because I don't want to lose him."

So God reveals His glory in answered prayer. That is one reason why we ought to pray—so that we can see God's glory and give Him praise. People who never pray really cut God off from one of the ways by which He wants to gain glory.

Speak It Out. The tenth way by which we may glorify God is by proclaiming His Word. God wants to communicate to men. How does He communicate? In the Book. Now when I take His Word and communicate it to you, then you are getting the mind of God. Consequently, He is glorified because He is able to speak to you. And when you communicate the Word, you are glorifying God.

Paul wrote, "Finally, brethren, pray for us, that the word of the Lord may have free course, and be glorified, even as it is with you" (2 Thessalonians 3:1). How was the Word glorified in them? Because they heard and believed it. They got saved and God got the glory. People hear God speaking in His Word and they respond.

If I enter the pulpit only to give my opinions, God would not get the glory. People might go out saying, "Isn't John MacArthur clever?" Well, let me tell you, I know from personal acquaintance that he isn't! He has to spend enough hours each day just trying to figure out what God is saying, let alone add any of his own clever thoughts. But if the Word is proclaimed, people leave saying, "Isn't God wonderful!" That brings glory to Him.

A further illustration: "And when the Gentiles heard this, they were glad, and glorified the word of the Lord. . ." (Acts 13:48). They heard Paul preach, and they gave glory to God.

Presenting the Word, then, gives Him glory. Every time you get in that class of kids or teach a Bible study in your home—or every time you sit down with your family and start talking about the Word of God—you are giving God glory. You honor Him by the word you speak when it is His Word.

This Way, Please!   Then—and this is number eleven on the list—we glorify God by bringing others to Him. God gets glory when people get saved. He is glorified when Satan's prison is broken open and men and women are turned loose from the power of Satan. God wants a great number of people giving Him glory. And so the more people who get converted, the more thanksgiving is going on; and the more thanksgiving going on, the more there are in the choir singing, "Hallelujah!" That's the idea. (*See* 2 Corinthians 4:15.)

God's glory shines from many angles in the salvation of souls. For one thing, when somebody gets saved, that individual gives Him glory. For another thing, when someone gets saved, the rest of us who already know the Lord give Him glory. When somebody comes along and says, "Say, I must tell you, my husband [or so and so] for whom we've been in prayer came to know Christ this week!" We say, "Praise the Lord!" We give glory to God. So not only is there another individual who has been added to the choir of the "Hallelujah Chorus," but many believers praise God as well.

God is going to display saved people, in heaven as a sign of His wisdom to the angels forever (Ephesians 3:10). We're going to be God's trophies in heaven. All through eternity God will point to us and say, "See how wise I am, angels?" And they're going to reply, "Yes! Anybody who could bring that bunch to such heights—yes, Lord, that's wisdom!"

Listen to Ephesians 1:12: "That we should be to the praise of his glory, who first trusted in Christ." Why does God give us an inheritance?—*for the praise of His glory.* Why does He give us the Holy Spirit, who is the guarantor of our inheritance until the redemption is finally carried out? ". . . unto the praise of his glory" (v. 14). You are saved to give God glory—that is the purpose of your existence. That is the reason you are a Christian. And if you really want to give Him glory, you are going to be involved not only in praising Him, but in winning others to Jesus Christ.

Glorify God by Sexual Purity.   In 1 Corinthians 6:18 Paul says to "flee fornication." He gives three reasons why a Christian's liberty never was meant to allow sexual sin. Sexual sin harms, enslaves, and perverts (*see* vv. 12–20).

When a Christian sins sexually, God is dishonored because our bodies are for the Lord, one with Christ, and sanctuaries of the Holy Spirit. Sexual sin joins the Lord to a prostitute, Paul exclaims! God is dishonored, the temple desecrated. So it is unthinkable to use Christ's body for sexual sin.

A friend of mine said that he once saw a unique shrine in a Catholic church. It had a sign over it saying, "This shrine is out of order, do not worship here." That sign would have to be hung on an immoral Christian.

Paul closes the section by saying, "Glorify God in your body" (*see* v. 20). We are to run from the trap of sex as Joseph ran from the arms of Potiphar's wife when she tried to seduce him (Genesis 39). And God will be glorified through our purity as clean sanctuaries.

One in Him.   One last way to glorify God—we give God glory by our unity. If I were to pinpoint one single tragedy that has marred the testimony of the church in the world, it would be the division, conflict, discord, dissension, and disunity among us. No wonder the world has no clear understanding of the validity of Christianity when some of the biggest battles going on in the world are between Christians. The Bible says we are to love one another, that the world may know we belong to Jesus Christ. So it commands us, for example, not even to take a brother to law before a pagan judge. Why? In order that the world might see unity of mind and purpose in the church.

Let me amplify this. Romans 15:5 tells us, "Now the God of patience and consolation grant you to be likeminded one toward another according to Christ Jesus." Now our example is always Christ, right? What does it mean to be "likeminded" as this verse instructs? It means that there is to be no preference in how I treat people—nonpreferential love. Jesus was "likeminded" in that He treated everybody the same. God expects that of us: "That ye may with one mind and one mouth glorify God . . ." (v. 6). Paul admonished the Corinthians, "Now I beseech you, brethren, by the name of our Lord Jesus Christ, that ye all speak the same thing, and that there be no divisions among you; but that ye be perfectly joined together in the same mind and in the same judgment (1 Corinthians 1:10).

Now there is room for different views on minor matters, but not for different views on the cardinal doctrines of the Word of God. We may differ on educational issues, on economic matters, on politics, but we must stand with one mind and one mouth to declare a united front for Jesus Christ.

People will take notice. God is not the "author of confusion." When an unbeliever sees confusion, he assumes that the One God must not be at work there. So God wants unity. Instead of shutting people out of our little group because they don't do all the things we do, we receive them because Christ has received them. We do this " . . . to the glory of God" (Romans 15:7). God is glorified when there is unity among the brethren, as in the words of the song—"They will know we are Christians by our love."

The End Result: Joy.   We've looked at a dozen ways by which we may glorify our Father in heaven. All that falls under the first part of the catechism statement: *The chief end of man is to glorify God.* But now let's turn briefly to the last part of that famous statement—*and to enjoy Him forever.* When we live to glorify God, He responds by giving us overwhelming joy. I sometimes think that if I were any happier and had more joy, I would not be able to stand it. Life becomes thrilling in response to glorifying God.

"Well, I've got a tough life. I just don't have any joy," you say. May I suggest an answer? Just start glorifying God. Like Habakkuk of old, your circumstances may not change, but *you* will change. He declared, " . . . I will joy in the God of my salvation" (Habakkuk 3:18). It took him an entire chapter to recite everything he knew about God, but then he came out rejoicing. That is the pattern. Live to the glory of God, and joy will come.

When you see a brother without joy, you know he is not making it in the Christian life. God never expects believers to be ugly, depressed, blighted. He wants us to be joyous even in the midst of trouble. Jesus said, "These things have I spoken unto you, that my joy might remain in you, and that your joy might be full" (John 15:11).

That is hard to do, because your joy fades, and so does mine. Then what can we do? Get down on our knees and confess the sin in our lives. Sin steals joy. We need to pray, "Restore unto me the joy of thy salvation . . ." (Psalms 51:12). Then we yield to the Holy Spirit and joy comes. Do you know that being filled with the Spirit and having joy is the same thing? The fruit of the Spirit is joy—one of them, at least. Joy is the by-product of living a Spirit-controlled life. Acts 13:52 tells us that the disciples were filled with joy and with the Holy Spirit. The two go together. "For the kingdom of God is not food and drink, but righteousness, and peace, and joy in the Holy Spirit" (*see* Romans 14:17). The Spirit-filled life brings its own built-in joy.

Now and Forever.   The catechism says that we will enjoy God forever. We can know God and enjoy Him now. We can have joy in God now *and* in the future. Listen to the marvelous words of Psalms 73:25: "Whom have I in heaven but thee? and there is none upon earth that I desire beside thee." The Psalmist was excited about enjoying God—and enjoying Him in the hereafter. Our joy in heaven will be the same as what we experience here. Heaven will be the full expression of that joy, totally unencumbered by sin.

Jesus prayed, "That my joy might remain in you" (*see* John 15:11). His joy that we know now is what we will know perfectly in heaven.The greatest promise in the Bible is found in 1 Thessalonians 4:17: " . . . so shall we ever be with the Lord." That's joy.

The chief end of man is to glorify God—and to enjoy Him forever!—a very old key to spiritual growth, but it always clicks the lock.

3

Obedience—
Unlocking the Servants' Quarters

A few years ago I met an incredible man—Fred D——. He became known as the Great Imposter, remember? A book and a movie were based on his life bacause of the many occupations he pursued without any qualifications. He served as a university executive, as a psychologist, as a Texas assistant prison warden, as a Canadian navy surgeon in Korea—and as a teacher in my high school, probably the best teacher there! He would falsify evidence, forge identity papers, and perform functions which appeared to confirm his claim to be something he wasn't.

This very thing takes place in the church all the time. The church is loaded with imposters such as Matthew 13 warns about in the parable of the Wheat and Tares (vv. 36–43). All this brings up an interesting and vital question. How can you tell if a person is a genuine Christian or a fake Christian? There are a number of criteria, but among the most important is the matter of obedience. A person may say, "Oh, yes, I believe, I believe, I believe." But then he lives his life giving no obedience to the One he professes with his lips as Lord. Something is wrong—terribly wrong. It doesn't match up. Our Saviour asked, "And why call ye me, Lord, Lord, and do not the things which I say?" (Luke 6:46).

People have a right to be suspicious of one who says he believes in Jesus but fails to reveal anything happening in his life to support the genuineness of his so-called faith. James declared that faith must radiate itself in certain deeds, in order to be valid visibly. If you really believe God, then there will be evidence of it in the way you live, in the things you say, and in the things you do. So there is an inseparable relationship between obedience and faith—almost like two sides of a coin. It is difficult to discuss one without including the other. You grow spiritually while you obey—obedient children who grow to be mature, obedient, and productive adults.

Noah: Proof Positive.   We might turn to a number of characters in the Bible to illustrate a faith that obeys, but I can think of no greater example than Noah. He is the classic of all classics of believing God, of saying, "I have faith and I'll do something to prove it." Noah took one further step than the earlier examples of faith, Abel and Enoch. The record of Abel shows us the worship of God. The record of Enoch shows us the walk with God. And the record of Noah shows us the work for God. Noah worshiped, walked, *and* worked. You've got to have *worship* before you have walk, and you've got to have *walk* before you have *work*. That is how God has established it.

Noah's faith and obedience go so far beyond human rationale that it does not even make sense to the normal mind. Unless a man knew God and had some kind of spiritual insight, he would be a blithering idiot to do what Noah did. Noah couldn't see anything beyond his own trust, but that was enough for him. And his life of believing and of obeying may be summed up in two areas. First, *he responded to God's Word.* Second, *he rebuked the world.*

1. Respond to God's Word.   "By faith Noah, being warned of God of things not seen as yet, moved with fear, prepared an ark to the saving of his house . . ." (Hebrews 11:7). He believed God—so much so that he built an ark. Now it may appear on the surface that Noah was somewhat foolhardy. Why did he do what he did? Because God said to him, "Noah, judgment is coming. I'm going to destroy the world by water. You'd better build a boat." So Noah dropped everything and spent more than a hundred years obeying God's command.

I don't know about you, but after seventy or eighty years, I'd begin to wonder. After all, Noah lived in Mesopotamia between the Tigris and Euphrates rivers, miles and miles from any ocean. But that's faith responding to God's Word. And mature faith doesn't question—it just obeys.

Now Noah was a human being, just as we are. He had a lot of things to do to occupy his time. For him to give up such a great block of his life to construct a huge boat took some kind of commitment. He listened to God, and then he spent his life obeying what God said. Isn't that amazing? It would have been one thing for him to run out and secure the lumber, but it was something else to see him a hundred years later still putting on the pitch. Some of us believe God, and we run out and start, but that's that. We never get much past that point. Noah continued in his obedience. Jesus said that this was the mark of a true child of His (John 8:31).

By faith Noah, being warned. . . . The words *of God* don't appear in some of the manuscripts, but they certainly should be included, if not in the text, then in parentheses, because obviously it was God who spoke. Noah was absolutely convinced of the authority which lay behind the command to him. One warning was enough.

"Aha!" you say. "That's why Noah did it. God held a big stick over him and said, 'You'd better do this or I'll let you have it.' " No, that's not it. The word *fear* gives an erroneous impression that he was under the influence of fright. But the Greek word means "to reverence." Noah obeyed because he reverenced God's Word. The implication is that Noah acted with pious care. He treated the message of God with great reverence and prepared the ark for saving not only himself, but also his wife, his three sons, Shem, Ham, and Japheth, and their three wives.

Now let's go back to Genesis 6 and see some of the fascinating things that took place. "Make thee an ark of gopher wood; rooms shalt thou make in the ark, and shalt pitch it within and without with pitch" (v. 14). That was a challenge to faith and obedience on an absolutely unprecedented scale. What would you do if God told you to build a 20,000-ton ship in the middle of the wilderness? One of the greatest acts of obedience in the history of the world took place when Noah stretched out his arms and chopped down the first tree.

I can't resist a digression from our subject. Though you may

be tempted to hurry on, stop to look closely at the word *pitch.*
That word *(kapher)* in Hebrew is exactly the same word translated "atonement." It can be either. Leviticus 17:11 might read
this way: "For the life of the flesh is in the blood: and I have
given it to you upon the altar [to be pitch] for your souls: for
it is the blood that [serves as pitch] for the soul." In the ark of
safety, the pitch kept the waters of judgment out. And the pitch
in the life of the believer is the blood of Christ which secures
us from any judgment. There can be no leaks in the ark because
of the pitch, and the judgment of God can never touch the
believer because the blood of Christ has sealed him from the
flood of judgment. What a great symbolism!

Size—"And this is the fashion which thou shalt make it of: The
length of the ark shall be three hundred cubits, the breadth of
it fifty cubits, and the height of it thirty cubits (Genesis 6:15).
God gave Noah a verbal blueprint. As you may know, there is
quite a bit of variation in how much an ancient cubit measured,
since it took as its standard the distance between a man's elbow
and finger. In general terms, the dimensions of the ark would
be about 450 feet long, 75 feet wide, and 45 feet high—about
the height of a four-story building. Since the ark had 3 decks,
its total area was approximately 95,000 square feet. That would
be more than 20 standard-size basketball courts. That's big! Its
size places it well within the category of large, steel, ocean-
going vessels of our modern world. As far as we can tell, it was
similar to a covered raft—shaped like a coffin—rather square
and flat-bottomed.

An instructor once gave a lecture to admirals at Annapolis
Naval Academy. "For centuries," this man said, "men built
ships in various proportions. But since British naval machinists
found the formula for the battleship *Dreadnaught,* all naval
construction follows the proportions of *Dreadnaught,* since
they have been found to be scientifically perfect." Then he
added, "The proportions of *Dreadnaught* are exactly the same
as the ark." So God knew how to build ships.

Weather Forecast: Rain—"And, behold, I, even I, do bring a
flood of waters upon the earth, to destroy all flesh, wherein is

the breath of life, from under heaven; and every thing that is in the earth shall die" (Genesis 6:17). That must have been difficult for Noah to understand. Noah had no concept of rain, since it had never rained upon the earth (Genesis 2:5). A mist from the earth, the next verse says, watered the whole face of the ground. So there were not even any deserts then.

Some scientists believe that the whole earth was enshrouded in a watery canopy, and it was this condition that enabled men to live for so long. Harmful rays of the sun did not penetrate this vapor and so the process of deterioration was greatly slowed down. But after the Flood—with the breaking up of the fountains of the deep and the crashing down of all that water stored up above the earth (Genesis 7:11)—this sudden and dramatic change of atmosphere resulted in an immediate shortening of man's life-span.

No Converts—Now the Flood that God told Noah would come was a long way off—120 years, in fact (Genesis 6:3). Noah could easily have rationalized and said, "Well, that sure gives people a lot of time to repent and to reform. They'll surely shape up by then." But what did Noah do during these long years? He preached. Every day he preached, but nobody believed him. As a preacher myself, I know that must have been hard to take. Yet Noah kept right on giving out the message.

Oh, perhaps, just perhaps, Noah began to question. He may have begun to think, "I wonder if there's something wrong with me? I've gone over this sermon many, many times, and nobody buys it." You can well imagine what this man of obedience must have endured as he pounded and preached. People passing by would point to him, touch their heads, and say, "There's that crazy Noah."

And perhaps he would think to himself, "Even if the Flood does come, how is this monster going to float—especially with all the different kinds of animals in it? It has no anchor, no mast, no steering, no rudder, no sail—not much of anything except size." But through it all, Noah believed God and obeyed him.

The Promise—"But with thee will I establish my covenant . . ." (Genesis 6:18). God said, in effect, "Noah, you're going to

be My man and I'm going to maintain My promise to you."
What was the basis for this promise? "But Noah found grace in
the eyes of the Lord" (v. 8). Now the grace wasn't in Noah—it
lay in the eyes of the Lord. Grace is strictly God's to give to
whom He will. Noah was no different from any other son of
Adam. Later, after the Flood, he would sin tragically (Genesis
9:21). But the grace of God was extended to Noah because God
wished to do so. It pleased the Lord to be gracious to Noah—to
spare him and to make a covenant with him.

"And of every living thing of all flesh, two of every sort shalt
thou bring into the ark, to keep them alive with thee; they shall
be male and female. Of fowls after their kind, and of cattle after
their kind, of every creeping thing on the earth after his kind,
two of every sort shall come unto thee, to keep them alive. And
take thou unto thee of all food that is eaten, and thou shalt
gather it to thee; and it shall be for food for thee, and for them"
(Genesis 6:19–21).

That's an extended way of saying, "Now, after you've built
this boat, I want to get the animals into it and provide for their
care." Imagine, if you can, the day this was all fulfilled. Noah
just sat at the gangplank, waiting for all those animals to come
in from everywhere. He did not have to go out and round them
up; they just came. There is no way to explain that fact other
than that it was God herding them into this big boat.

It's been calculated from a spatial standpoint that the ark
could easily have handled 7,000 species of animals. That's quite
a number! It doesn't necessarily mean two of every animal in
the world, since one basic species can generate a wide variety
of animals. All horses, for instance, whether Shetland ponies,
racing horses, draft animals, or whatever, are descended from
one common ancestor. Two cows could well have represented
the whole bovine family. So it is very likely that the species
were limited. It is within reason to assume there was plenty of
room for all the species on board. It has been estimated that
there is a total of about 2,500 animal species—the average size
being that of a cat, which would require less than two square
feet of living space. So it was no problem to get the animals into

the ark from a logistics standpoint. But that still left the matter of the feeding and care of this great number of animals. Who would feed them? How would the sanitation problem be cared for? You can see the enormous problems of a trip to last a year.

Total Obedience—But Noah was a man of obedience, so he began to build. "Thus did Noah; according to all that God commanded him, so did he" (v. 22). What faith! Total obedience! How unlike most of us. God says to us, "I want you to take this ministry, or I want you to reach that person over there, or I want you to trust Me in the trial that you're going through." Yet how often we fail to obey God in these situations, let alone build an ark. We say we believe, but our faith is absolutely infinitesimal in relation to that of Noah. And some of us run out of patience very quickly. We obey for a week. Noah obeyed for 120 years.

What were the grounds for his obedience? God's Word. He believed that God meant what He said about judgment and what He said about His promise. So Noah built the ark exactly as he was supposed to. He obeyed God to the very letter. He didn't pick and choose his points of obedience. Some people want to believe God about promise, but not about judgment —but we must believe both equally.

Charles Spurgeon said, "He who does not believe that God will punish sin, will not believe that He will pardon it through atoning blood. I charge you who profess the Lord not to be unbelieving with regard to the terrible threatenings of God to the ungodly. Believe the threat, even though it should chill your blood. Believe, though nature shrinks from the overwhelming doom, for if you do not believe, the act of disbelieving God at one point will drive you to disbelieve upon the other points."

So Noah believed God—believed not only the promise of safety in the ark, but also in the imminent destruction of the world. He believed both. He believed God totally.

2. Rebuke the World.   The first thing, then, that solidified his faith is that he believed and responded to God's Word. The second point is that Noah's obedience rebuked the world. Hebrews 11:7 tells us, "By faith Noah, being warned of God of things not seen as yet, moved with fear, prepared an ark to the saving of his house; by the which he condemned the world. . . ." Now it is true that Noah was a "preacher of righteousness," but just how did he preach? By building an ark. That was his sermon. Every time passersby saw him, heard him chop down a tree, or looked up at him walking along with a plank on his back—each person heard or was seeing a sermon enacted. And it was saying, "Judgment is coming. Judgment is coming. Judgment is coming." Yet no one believed—not during those long 120 years.

Not even the carpenters assisting Noah accepted his message. Noah must have hired many of the men of the town to help him and his sons because they alone could never have carried the massive timbers they used in the construction of the ark. But though they helped him build it, they were not saved by it. They took their weekly paychecks, but then perished in the Flood. Likewise today there are people assisting in building the church by their labor and by their gifts, but still they are lost and will perish because they are not secure in Christ.

"Was God being too severe with them?" you may wonder. Well, Genesis 6:5 tells us what kind of people they were. "And God saw that the wickedness of man was great in the earth, and that every imagination of the thoughts of his heart was only evil continually." Each one was vile on the inside, and God saw it all. "I know the things that come into your mind" (*see* Ezekiel 11:5)—God reads the heart.

But God's heart was also involved. "And it repented the Lord that he had made man on the earth, and it grieved him at his heart" (Genesis 6:6). Does that mean that God changed His mind? Was He taken by surprise? No, this is an anthropomorphism—a statement about God in human terms. From a human standpoint, it appears as if God repented. But 1 Samuel 15:29 tells us, "And also the Strength of Israel will not lie nor repent; for he is not a man, that he should repent."

God's Judgment.   From God's perspective, nothing had changed. But humanly speaking, it appears as though God had changed His mind and had decided to erase the race. "And the Lord said, I will destroy man whom I have created from the face of the earth, both man, and beast, and the creeping thing, and the fowls of the air; for it repenteth me that I have made them" (Genesis 6:7).

That was a very serious solution to the problem. But the race was largely demon-possessed. When the Bible says that the sons of God cohabited with the daughters of men, I believe the reference applies to fallen angels. Demons having sexual relations with women produced a race that was offbeat and demonic. So God said, "I'm going to wipe out this rotten world. I'm going to judge it."

Was God too severe—was this the end of mercy? No, the fact that God's patience will end, the fact that He will strike out to judge—this is the only hope for a sin-cursed world. If God didn't act to destroy, then men would have had to live in a world of eternal sin and violence. And that would be terrible. My friend, we ought to be thankful that sin gets judged. God is holy and just, and He must set things right. But judgment comes only after God's great patience.

Man's Rejection.   Every man has enough knowledge of God so that he is without excuse (Romans 1:19, 20). From the time of Adam and Eve, God had promised a Redeemer (Genesis 3:15). From that time on, the expiatory sacrificial system was in effect. Mankind knew how to come to God. Adam lived 930 years, and perhaps spent most of that time telling men the truth about what sin had done to him and to the world. The preaching of Enoch served as a warning, as did the preaching of Noah. But there came a time when the Spirit of God no longer tried to make the case. The people knew the truth, but they just rejected it. Noah's life of obedience stood out in bold relief as an open rebuke to the men of his time.

Is that very different from our own day? Our Lord said, "But as the days of [Noah] were, so shall also the coming of the Son of man be" (Matthew 24:37). Noah preached and people laughed, as people now snicker at the proclamation of the Gospel. The Holy Spirit was through striving then as He will be through in the future when the church is taken away at the Rapture. But in Noah's day a remnant found grace, and so today people are being saved by the grace of God—saved not from a judgment of water, but from a judgment of fire. God needs more men and women like Noah—those who will obey God no matter how bizarre or strange or difficult the command may be.

Motivating Obedience.   As great an example as Noah was, however, we can't leave this subject of obedience without updating it by a New Testament concept. This will round out our understanding of obedience as a key to growth. Remember that we began this chapter by suggesting that one way to tell whether or not a person was a genuine Christian or a fake Christian was by the measure of obedience. But what is the motivating force of that obedience? What kind of obedience is it? Let's see if we can find out from the Book of 1 John.

"And hereby we do know that we know him, if we keep his commandments" (1 John 2:3). Now the word *keep* carries the idea of "watchful, observant obedience." But it is not an obedience connected particularly with force or pressure. We do not say, "Well, I have to obey because if I don't I'll get whacked by the divine hammer." *No, it isn't that at all.* It's more like, "I can't wait to do this!"

Alford's *Greek Testament* defines *keep* as "to watch or guard or to keep, as some precious thing." The true Christian demonstrates that he knows God by the great desire of his heart to guard obedience. The habitual, moment-by-moment safeguarding of the Word of God in a spirit of obedience is the sign of a mature Christian. When people claim to be Christians and live any way that they want, in complete disregard for God's commandments, they undermine their claim.

The word which John uses here for "commandment" is also significant. In this book John uses the word *entolē* at least fourteen times, referring to the precepts of Christ. But in the Gospel when John speaks of the law of Moses, he uses a different word—*nomos*. John wants to emphasize the precepts of Christ rather than the law of Moses. If we have a spirit of obedience toward the safeguarding of the precepts of Christ, a consuming desire that they be honored, and a determination to obey them, this constitutes continuing experiential proof that a person has come to the knowledge of God and the Lord Jesus Christ.

Now when a person becomes a Christian, he openly acknowledges that Jesus is his Lord. And if he really enthrones Christ, then he gladly submits to His authority. Obedience is a foregone conclusion. If a person says to Jesus, "You are Lord!" that settles the question. Those who continue to keep His commandments are the ones who are really knowing God and assured of it.

Two Kinds of Obedience.   But what if we try to be obedient, and fail—are we condemned? I have struggled with this problem long enough so that I think I can help you understand it. We must distinguish between *legal* obedience and *gracious* obedience. Legal obedience pertains to the covenant of works. Legal obedience demands an absolute, perfect obedience without a single failure. If you violate the law even once—death! That is the pain and the failure of legal obedience.

But there is such a thing as gracious obedience, and even the words themselves sound better. Gracious obedience pertains to the covenant of grace. This is a loving and sincere spirit of obedience which, though filled with defects, is nevertheless accepted by God, for its blemishes are blotted out by the blood of Jesus Christ.

See the difference? In the grace covenant, God looks at the heart, not at the works. I'm glad, aren't you? If God were measuring me on legal obedience, I would spend eternity in hell. But God looks at me and says, in effect, "MacArthur, with all your defects, you have a heart that is tending to be obedient to Me. You have a spirit that wills to submit to My Lordship, even though you frequently fail."

That is why we are blessed to be on this side of the cross. Jesus died so that His blood can take care of the defects of obedience. It is far better to be under gracious obedience than under legal obedience.

The Heart's Desire.   Lest anyone get the wrong idea, let me illustrate. Did the disciples always—always—legally obey God? Of course they didn't. Take Peter, for example, or James or John. All failed the Lord and made mistakes, sinful men that they were. Yet Jesus could say, "Father, they have obeyed thy word" (*see* John 17:6). Had they? Consistently? They would have blushed at the very suggestion. Now, was Jesus measuring them by an absolute Mosaic legal obedience, or was He measuring their obedient spirit? You know the answer—their propensity, their desire, their determination to submit to Jesus Christ—that's what Jesus measured, and He covered their defects by His shed blood.

God is not expecting absolute perfection. If you do something wrong or fail, He doesn't say you are finished and no longer a Christian. No, God is looking at the constant flow of a heart that has in it the spirit of obedience. The true Christian has a desire to submit to Jesus Christ even though he cannot always make that desire come to pass. But God reads and accepts it.

Such obedience is based not on law but on love, not on fear but on friendship. Several verses in John point this out. As Jesus was telling of His soon return to heaven, He did not say, "Now keep My commandments—or else." Rather, "He that hath my commandments, and keepeth them, he it is that loveth me . . ." (John 14:21). So we obey—not because we fear—but because we love.

Non-Christians, of course, know nothing of this gracious obedience. Instead of submitting themselves to the Lordship of Christ, they go about trying to crank out their own righteousness, and by that act are damning themselves under legal obedience. "They profess that they know God; but in works they deny him . . ." (Titus 1:16). They make the profession, but, unlike Noah, their works don't back them up. At the Great White Judgment Throne many people are going to say, "Lord, Lord, have we not done wonderful works in Your name?" But Jesus will answer, "Depart from Me, I never knew you."

There is no true knowledge of Christ that does not result in the spirit of gracious obedience.

The Pattern of Obedience.   We have, then, the principle that it is possible to identify a Christian because of his obedience. Now, let's go on to the pattern of obedience. By a pattern I mean something that you can put your life on and trace. First John 2:6 tells us: "He that saith he abideth in *him* ought himself also so to walk, even as *he* walked" (italics added). We may understand the word *abiding* as meaning knowing Him, walking in the light, being in fellowship, terms indicating salvation. The point is that if you declare that you are a Christian, you ought to be like Jesus.

You may say, "Oh, it was bad enough that we had to keep His commandments. Now we have to be like Him. I can't do it!" Well, the verse does not say that we *will* be exactly like Him, but that we *ought* to be like Him. Christ is our pattern. We are to move toward the likeness of Christ. We ought to live as He lived. Obedience moves us toward Christlikeness.

Take a couple of specifics. Philippians 2:8 tells us about Jesus: "And being found in fashion as a man, he humbled himself, and became obedient unto death, even the death of the cross." Jesus was in the form of God, but He did not insist on hanging on to that glory and privilege. Instead, He was willing to lay it aside temporarily and humble Himself. That is the greatest illustration of humility ever. And that is our pattern.

Note that this passage also speaks of Christ's obedience. Our Lord was obedient in everything. He paid His taxes. He obeyed the Mosaic Law to the very letter. He obeyed the ceremonial law. He obeyed the special divine stipulations of His Messiahship. John's Gospel makes this point very clear. Jesus said, "For I came down from heaven, not to do mine own will, but the will of him that sent me" (John 6:38). His whole spirit was obedience. Again, " . . . the Father hath not left me alone; for I do always those things that please him" (John 8:29). And in John 14:31: " . . . as the Father gave me commandment, even so I do. . . ." Again—obedience. Christ set the pattern. His loving obedience, then, becomes what we are to actually trace our lives after. This kind of obedience characterized our blessed Christ and it is to be true of us.

Your Record?   This chapter began with a reference to the Great Imposter. One day many years ago he came into my dad's study and began to talk about Christianity. My preacher-father handed him L. S. Chafer's multivolume work *Systematic Theology*—just as a starter. He devoured it in very short order. He became a Christian—not a fake one but a genuine believer.

Whether you realize it or not, people are looking at your life all the time. They are hearing the sermon your life proclaims. "Thus did Noah according to all that God commanded him, so did he" (Genesis 6:22). Will the same be said of you? You grow to be like Christ while you obey.

4

The Filling of the Spirit—
Unlocking the Power Plant

Fancy someone giving you a $10,000 automobile. You get the title and the keys. You walk out to the curb, slip behind the wheel, turn on the ignition—and nothing happens. You finally discover what's wrong. Your new car hasn't been filled with gas. So you don't go anywhere—until you get fueled up.

That's the way it is in the Christian life. In chapter 7 we will learn about all the great things we possess in Christ. That's the car. Then, the Book of Ephesians instructs us on how we are to live—we are to be different, to love, to walk in the light, to be wise. The fact is, however, that we simply cannot do it in our own strength and energy. We must have God's fuel, and that is the Person of the Holy Spirit. God has provided this great resource for practical Christian living. To try to function without the Holy Spirit is like owning Standard Oil and never having gas for the car.

As we consider this essential key to the Christian life, the filling of the Holy Spirit, let me point out a contrast, a command, and finally the consequences connected with this subject.

A Contrast: *Not With Wine.*   The contrast finds expression in Ephesians 5:18: "And be not drunk with wine, wherein is excess; but be filled with the Spirit."

All people like to be happy—to be exhilarated with joy, to feel good, and to be on top of everything. There is nothing wrong with that. The Bible says there is a time to laugh. Scripture talks about "shouting for joy," and "good tidings of great joy." It refers to "joy unspeakable and full of glory." God wants joyous, excited, happy, uplifted people. The problem lies in how this happiness is generated. Often it is artificially induced. You might expect in our modern world (where so much is artificial) that someone would get the idea of brewing up joy and placing it in a bottle. That is exactly what has been done! And today we have millions of Americans frantically seeking artificial joy at the bottom of a bottle.

Drunkenness, of course, occurs in all countries and cultures. America is facing a major epidemic of alcoholism. I once visited the jungles of Ecuador and had to avoid hitting drunk Indians on the road. Go to remote parts of Africa and you will see that the natives have something intoxicating to drink. Check out the Arabs in their tents in the middle of nowhere and you will find them drinking as well. All these people, even those "highly civilized," unable to find real happiness, look for it in a drunken stupor. But all they find is a cheap, false, damning, artificial substitute for real joy.

Sometimes Christians do the same thing, even way back to first-century times. The fruit of the vine would ferment into an alcoholic beverage. Since the water was not pure, the people lived on wine. Usually the wine was diluted with water, but undiluted "strong drink" was readily available. Naturally it would be easy for a Christian drinking wine as a daily part of his life to be tempted toward drunkenness. The Bible repeatedly calls drunkenness a sin and warns against it. For example, Paul excluded those who would linger long beside the wine bottle from being elders or deacons in the church (1 Timothy 3:3, 8). The Book of Proverbs makes many prohibitions against drunkenness.

What about today's contemporary society? A believer may say, "Well, I don't get drunk. I only drink a little bit. Isn't that okay?" This is really not our topic at hand, but let me give you what I call a "Christian wine list"—five key questions to ask yourself:

1. *Will it be habit-forming?* Paul said, "All things are lawful . . . but I will not be brought under the power of any" (1 Corinthians 6:12).
2. *Will it lead to dissipation?* Scripture calls drunkenness dissipation or excess (Ephesians 5:18).
3. *Will it offend a weaker brother?* If another believer follows my example and falls into sin, then I have been the occasion for his stumbling (Romans 14:21).
4. *Will it harm my Christian testimony?* Someone may look at me and think less of my Christian testimony because of what I do (Romans 14:16).
5. *Am I certain that it is right?* If not, I'd be partaking of a doubtful thing, and that would be sin (Romans 14:23).

But With the Holy Spirit. Now, if Christians are not to be artificially drunk with wine, then where are they to get true joy and happiness? Our Ephesians text speaks clearly enough: "Be filled with the Holy Spirit." Our thrills, our exhilaration, and our happiness are to result from being filled with the Spirit, not from being filled with wine.

This alternative may seem a little shocking—to be drunk with the Holy Spirit. It is a strange contrast. But the Bible bears this out in several places. In Luke 1:15, for example, in the prophecy regarding the birth of John the Baptist, we learn that he " . . . shall drink neither wine nor strong drink; and he shall be filled with the Holy [Spirit], even from his mother's womb." In other words, John will get his joy and motivating power, his fuel, not out of a bottle but through the filling of the Spirit of God.

How about Acts 2, which records the coming of the Holy Spirit upon the disciples on the day of Pentecost? When they went out and began to proclaim God's message, the unbelievers standing around said that these Christians were full of new wine (v. 13). They were suggesting that in order for people to be so happy, so jubilant, and so extraverted, they must be drunk. But Peter set them straight and insisted that instead of wine it was the Holy Spirit at work (vv. 15–18).

The third time this contrast appears is right here in our text.

Here is the idea: in both cases—either being drunk on wine or being filled with the Holy Spirit—there is a new kind of behavior pattern. It is a kind of joyous boldness and lack of inhibition. You know how a meek, mild type of person can become just the opposite when he gets drunk? His personality appears to change under the influence of alcohol. He becomes uninhibited. He doesn't seem to care what people think about him. He loses his restrictions and abandons himself to the effects of drink. Paul speaks precisely of this identical thing. We need to be totally abandoned to the control of the Holy Spirit so that our egos do not even play a part. We need to move around with the real exhilaration and the thrill and the joy that the unsaved seek artificially in wine.

So here is the contrast that the apostle gives. When we come under the control of the Holy Spirit, we live a different, free, uninhibited life, generated by the divine fuel—for God's glory.

A Command.   In addition to this contrast, our Ephesians text also gives us a command—the last part of the verse: "Be filled with the Spirit."

What does it mean to be Spirit-filled? First, let me point out something basic and exciting. Every Christian possesses the Holy Spirit. If you are a believer, the Spirit of God lives within you. Paul asked, "What? know ye not that your body is the temple of the Holy Spirit?" (*see* 1 Corinthians 6:19). The Spirit lives within you! ". . . if any man have not the Spirit of Christ, he is none of his," Paul emphasized in Romans 8:9. So all believers possess the Spirit. You do not have to ask for the Spirit. He is in you even as He has been since the time of your salvation.

Paul never says, "Be indwelt by the Spirit." The believer is already indwelt. Paul never says, "Be baptized in the Spirit." The believer was baptized into the body of Christ at the moment of his conversion (1 Corinthians 12:13). Paul never says, "Be sealed with the Spirit." The believer is already sealed. Your possession of the Spirit, your indwelling by the Spirit, your baptism by the Spirit, your sealing by the Spirit—all these positional things were accomplished at your salvation.

The thing Paul is saying here, in essence, is: "Be continually letting the Spirit of God, who is already in you, fill you." The Greek verb means "be continually filled," or "be kept filled." It is continuous action. It is not a second work of grace. It is not an added experience to run around and seek. It is simply to let the Spirit of God, who is already in you, fill you.

This truth can be checked out in the Book of Acts. Start with chapter 4 and run through chapter 13 and you will read repeatedly that the same disciples were filled here, filled there, filled on this circumstance and on that. We, too, need to be filled again and again as we yield control to the Holy Spirit. We never come to the place where we can say, "Well, I got the filling, so now I'm set." No, the filling of the Spirit is a continuing experience. We may be filled today, but tomorrow is a new opportunity.

Under the Influence.   We need to clarify precisely what is meant by *filled*. Some might hold the idea that it is like dumping something into a glass to fill it up. But that's not a good parallel. Let me give a better illustration (from "The Fizzie Principle" in my booklet *God's Will Is Not Lost*).

> A Fizzie is a small tablet used to make a soft drink; it's sort of a flavored Alka-Seltzer. Put it in a glass of water and its flavor releases throughout the water. This concentrated, compact power pill is no good as long as it sits on the bottom of the glass. It has to release its energy to fill the glass, and *then* it turns the water into something new. If it is a grape Fizzie, you get a glass of grape drink. The flavor of the tablet determines the flavor of the water.
>
> In a measure, that pictures how the Spirit of God operates in a human life. He is in the Christian all the time as a compact, concentrated, powerful force of divine energy. The question is, has He ever been able to release that power, to fill your life so that you can become what He is? A Christian not yielded to the Spirit of God does not manifest the Christ-life. The Spirit of God has to permeate a life if that life is to radiate Him.

We cannot do anything apart from being filled with the Spirit.

I have a glove. I say to the glove, "Play the piano." What does the glove do? Nothing. The glove cannot play the piano. But if I put my hand in the glove and play the piano, what happens? Music! (In my case it might be chaos, as I can't play the piano.) But if I put my hand in a glove, the glove goes. The glove does not get pious and say, "Oh, hand, show me the way to go." It does not say anything; it just goes. Spirit-filled people do not stumble and mumble around trying to find out what God wants. They just go!

People often ask, "How do I know my spiritual gift?" The best way is to live a Spirit-filled life, see what God does through you, look back in retrospect and say, "Oh, *that's* what I do when God has control of me. Apparently, that is my gift." There is no need to get analytical. The whole point is that we need the Spirit of God to be released in our lives. This is simply a matter of yielding, of *deciding* to turn one's life over to Him. Life is a matter of decisions. When you get up in the morning, you decide what you are going to wear. Next you decide what you are going to eat for breakfast. And so it goes through the day—one decision after another. The Spirit-filled life is yielding every decision to the control of the Spirit.

In a sense, that is how the Holy Spirit works or fills the Christian's life. He is already there, ready to explode with His potential power. Instead of the question, "Is He there?" the question becomes, "Has the Spirit been able to release the power to fill your life so that you will become like He is?" Being filled with the Spirit is to have the Holy Spirit released to permeate your life—to fill you in every dimension so that you become like Him.

To better understand what it means to be filled with the Holy Spirit, consider some New Testament passages which refer to other types of filling. In John 16:6, for example, after Jesus told His disciples that He was going away, they were filled with sorrow. That means they were consumed with sorrow. In Luke 6:11, after Jesus presented His claims as Messiah, the people were "filled with madness." They were totally captured by the feeling of rage. Acts 5:3 tells us that Ananias was full of Satan, meaning he was overwhelmed with the power of the evil one. So we see that the word *filled* signifies being totally captive to a particular emotion, power, or influence.

In Acts 4:31 we read, "And when they had prayed, the place was shaken where they were assembled together; and they were all filled with the Holy [Spirit], and they spake the word of God with boldness." They were consumed with the Spirit of God—with the emotion, the power, and the influence of the Holy Spirit. And so they could move out uninhibited, unmolded by their own egos, totally abandoned to communicate Jesus Christ.

The same can be true of us. We can be so captive to the Holy Spirit that we are abandoned to Him and crowd out all other emotions. The result is a great exhilaration, a thrilling happiness beyond any other that we might know. We can feel the Holy Spirit powerfully moving through our lives to our fullness of joy. We may react in different ways. We may cry. We may shout for joy. We may want to run around the block and just praise God. We may just want to sit in our room and thank Him. We may want to tell some other believer. In any case, when we are filled with the Spirit, we experience joy upon joy because He controls and captures every part of us.

The Means: Surrender.   To be filled with the Holy Spirit means to be totally under the influence of the Holy Spirit so that we are caught up in His direction, power, and energy. Now what about the *means* of filling? How does it happen? Very simple. It is just a matter of surrendering your will, your mind, your body, your time, your talents, your treasures, every single area of your life to the control of the Holy Spirit. It is just to say, "I want the Spirit of God to be Number One, to be the overwhelming controlling influence in my life."

To better understand what it means to be filled, consider a comparison. The Book of Ephesians lists some of the things that a Spirit-filled person does. A Spirit-filled person sings songs. The Spirit-filled wife submits to her husband. The Spirit-filled husband loves his wife. Spirit-filled children obey their parents. A Spirit-filled father does not provoke his children to wrath. A Spirit-filled employer is fair with his employees. All these are manifestations of the Spirit-filled life.

But now check Colossians 3:16: "Let the word of Christ dwell in you richly. . . . " What happens when that occurs? The very same thing that happens when you are filled with the Spirit (*see* vv. 16–23). Therefore, being filled with the Spirit is exactly the same thing as letting the Word of Christ dwell in you richly. They must be equal, for they produce the same thing.

Now let's go one step further for an additional comparison. To be Spirit-filled is to be Christ-conscious. It is practically the same thing as being deeply, richly involved in all that Jesus Christ is and what is said about Him. The truth which Jesus spoke—and the truth taught about Him—should govern every deed, every word, every hidden drive, every hidden motive, every desire of your heart. And as you study the Word of God, as you dwell in His Word, as it dwells in you richly, you become Christ-centered; you become Christ-conscious. That is just the same as being Spirit-filled.

To be filled with the Spirit means to live every moment as if you are standing in the presence of Jesus Christ. You can get up in the morning and in your heart say, "Good morning, Lord. It's Your day and I just want You to keep reminding me all day that You are right beside me." That is very practical. When Satan comes around, you can say, "Christ, I know You are in me. Get him! Lord, I'm being tempted and I need Your strength right now!"

It is also practical in making decisions. "Lord, I don't know which way to go. I've got two choices, two paths. Show me the way, Lord." If you are really Christ-conscious, you just bring Him in and let Him choose for you as you move through the day.

So we see that the filling of the Spirit is to live in a Christ-conscious way. Have you learned that? Do you habitually think of Jesus and acknowledge His presence in your life? That is to be Spirit-filled. Check out 2 Corinthians 3:18: "But we all, with open face beholding as in a glass the glory of the Lord, are changed into the same image from glory to glory even as by the Spirit of the Lord." You see, if you gaze at the Lord Jesus Christ and are unveiled with Him, the Spirit will make you into His very glorious image! That is the ultimate in spiritual growth and can only occur when we are totally absorbed in Him!

The Results.   We have looked at the *contrast* connected with the filling of the Spirit, and we have looked at the *command* to be filled with the Spirit. Now, what about the *consequences* of being filled with the Spirit?

Melody.   There are many, of course, but let us point out only two found in the context of our study. First, you'll sing. Ephesians 5:19 declares, "Speaking to yourselves in psalms and hymns and spiritual songs, singing and making melody in your heart to the Lord."

It doesn't matter whether you sing well aloud. The point is that you can make melody in your heart. And the fact that you do it internally may be a great blessing not only to you but to the rest of us as well! Do you know what it is to have a song in your heart? So many times people just sit in church and mumble, mumble, mumble. Sometimes they don't even try to sing. But if you are filled with the Spirit, you *do* sing. The Bible says so. How could it be otherwise if you have the joy and the exhilaration of the Spirit? As Spirit-filled Christians, we sing.

To whom do we sing? Our verse says "to yourselves." In the church we sing to each other. Sometimes the choir sings to us, and sometimes we all sing together. Sometimes somebody stands up and sings a testimony. All of us sing because of the joy produced by the filling of the Spirit. While doing this, we must be aware of the latent danger of singing artificially—of performing as a self-centered showcase and doing this for fleshly gratification, rather than out of the joy of a Spirit-filled life. A performance that does not express the Spirit-filled life is sin—because it stems from the desire for self-glory.

In addition to singing to each other, we sing to the Lord. Do you know that the Lord loves to hear you sing when you are giving expression to the joy of the Spirit? Music is the language of the emotions. How wonderful to be able to express your innermost self directly to the Saviour! If this is not the true expression of a sincere heart, and backed by a righteous life, God is not pleased (Amos 5:23, 24).

Now, what are we supposed to sing? According to our verse, we sing *psalms*—songs drawn directly from Scripture. We also sing *hymns*—the kind which the disciples sang in the upper room the night before our Lord suffered and died. And last, *spiritual songs*—deep, personal, emotional expressions of our testimony. The phrase "and making melody" is translated from the Greek word *psallō* which means "to pluck the lyre." Evidently we can also express our joy with instruments. Whether instrumentally or vocally, however, our reason for musical expression is the overwhelming joy of the Holy Spirit filling us.

Add Your Thanks.   In addition to singing, there is a further consequence of being Spirit-filled: the giving of thanks. Ephesians 5:20 says, "Giving thanks always for all things unto God and the Father in the name of our Lord Jesus Christ." The Spirit-filled, God-conscious Christian gives thanks for everything. We are long on our demands, yes, even our complaints—but we are short on our thanksgivings.

But if this is true, it is no fault of that singularly sunny and praiseful spirit among the early Christians—the Apostle Paul. For him it can be said that gratitude was far more a matter of principle than emotion, far more an affair of duty than of ecstasy. Wherever Paul went, he appeared in what one of the eloquent prophets calls "the garment of praise" (*see* Isaiah 61:3). There are some people who, if they ever wear thankfulness at all, wear it as you do a boutonniere—on Mother's Day or at a wedding. But not Paul! He wore gratitude as a man wears his everyday suit. Praise was woven into the fabric of his life. He wanted it to be so with his Christian brethren everywhere. So strong was his insistence on this point that he laid it down emphatically to the Christians in the Colossian church: " . . . be ye thankful" (Colossians 3:15).

In the story of the ten lepers whom Jesus healed, only one returned to give thanks (Luke 17:11–19). Thanksgiving is still outnumbered at least nine to one—a magnificent minority. Thanksgiving is not an act; it is an attitude. "And let the peace of Christ rule in your hearts, to which indeed you were called in one body; and be thankful" (Colossians 3:15 NAS). Gratitude fills the soul with the sunshine of God. Ingratitude keeps the soul's windows darkened, shutting out the light of God, turning life into a fog. For the Christian, every circumstance should be cause for thanksgiving.

Benjamin Franklin said, "In a time of great despondency among the first settlers of New England, it was proposed in one of their assemblies to proclaim a fast. An old farmer rose, reviewed their mercies, and proposed that, instead of provoking heaven with their complaints, they appoint a thanksgiving." We might learn a great lesson from that!! For every complaint we have, there is a multiple of things for which we could give thanks. Whatever our losses are here on this earth, we know that as Christians we shall someday receive our divine, eternal inheritance in glory—and for this we can always be thankful.

Jesus even said that "your sorrow shall be turned into joy" (*see* John 16:20). Here he used the example of a woman having a child. The pain is agonizing, but when the child is born, there is unequaled joy. So, for us, the very event that is causing sorrow will bring joy—so you can thank Him and rejoice in advance. The Spirit will produce this thanksgiving! Like the Prophet Habakkuk, you may not understand, but you praise God anyway.

THINGS FOR WHICH TO BE THANKFUL

Gifts From God—1 Timothy 4:3, 4

> Forbidding to marry, and commanding to abstain from meats, which God hath created to be received with thanksgiving of them which believe and know the truth. For every creature of God is good, and nothing to be refused, if it be received with thanksgiving.

God's Presence—Psalms 75:1, 9

> Unto thee, O God, do we give thanks, unto thee do we give thanks: for that thy name is near thy wondrous works de-

clare. . . . But I will declare for ever; I will sing praises to the God of Jacob.

Salvation—Romans 6:17

But God be thanked, that ye were the servants of sin, but ye have obeyed from the heart that form of doctrine which was delivered you.

Victory Over Death—1 Corinthians 15:57

But thanks be to God, which giveth us the victory through our Lord Jesus Christ.

Victory in Life—2 Corinthians 2:14

Now thanks be unto God, which always causeth us to triumph in Christ, and maketh manifest the savour of his knowledge by us in every place.

Generally in Everything—Philippians 4:6

Be careful for nothing; but in every thing by prayer and supplication with thanksgiving let your requests be made known unto God.

Spiritual Maturity.   It is only possible in the Christian life to be either Spirit-controlled or controlled by the flesh. The Apostle Paul called it by the terms *spiritual* and *carnal*. Growth toward Christ's likeness occurs *only* when you are spiritual, walking in the Spirit, filled by the Spirit. When you are carnal, you shift into neutral and go nowhere.

"And I, brethren, could not speak to you as to spiritual men, but as to men of flesh, as to babes in Christ. I gave you milk to drink, not solid food; for you were not yet able to receive it. Indeed, even now you are not yet able" (1 Corinthians 3:1, 2 NAS). Paul tells the Corinthians that he cannot feed them solid food which will cause them to grow mature, because their carnality has eliminated their spiritual teeth and they must suck only milk. Growth is retarded by carnality. Growth can only come when you are allowing the Spirit to produce energy. So the more frequently you are filled, the faster the rate of growth!

And maturity will result from the decreasing frequency of carnal times and the increase of spiritual times. Fuel up, friend, and head for the prize—to be made like Christ.

5

Confession—
Unlocking the Chamber of Horrors

David was a ladies' man. When he wanted a lady, he took her and it didn't matter whom she belonged to. At the height of his power, David became infatuated with the wife of one of his military officers—Bathsheba was her name—and he made her pregnant. He decided to solve the resulting problem by arranging for her husband to lead a suicide squad into the midst of a battle. He did—and was killed. Conveniently forgetting his intrigue, David gave the man a military funeral and proceeded to marry the pregnant wife. God relates the whole story in 2 Samuel 11.

By his actions David had broken four of the Ten Commandments: he had coveted, he had stolen, he had committed adultery, and he had murdered. Now a man with any moral sense, certainly a man who knows God, is going to be troubled, is going to be unnerved over such sin. And one day guilt caught up with David. He became obsessed with his sin. He could not get his sin out of his heart or out of his mind, and he could not get it off his hands.

So in his great outpouring of confession, Psalm 51, David prayed for four things. Sin had made him dirty, and he asked to be cleansed. Guilt had made him physically sick, and he asked to be healed. Iniquity had broken his joy with God, and he asked it to be restored. He knew he had directly violated God's love and laws, and he asked for pardon and mercy.

The whole subject of confession of sin is much discussed today, and I think it needs to be seen in the biblical perspective.

Confession is ever and always the pattern of the Christian's life and constitutes one of the essential keys to spiritual growth.

Cover-Up Results.   Christians today face the same dilemma that David faced—whether to try to cover up the sin, as he attempted to do for an entire year—or whether to confess and be done with it. We have all fought this battle. I can remember in my own childhood confronting the matter head-on time after time. My mother would come in and line up all four children against the wall and say, "All right, which one of you did it?" To admit or not to admit—that was the question! You know, of course, that this is a recurring issue all through life.

Now what can be said for the one who covers up—or tries to? For one thing, there is lack of prosperity. "He that covereth his sins shall not prosper . . ." (Proverbs 28:13). Physical illness is another result of covering up. David testified, "When I kept silence, my bones waxed old through my roaring all the day long. For day and night thy hand was heavy upon me . . ." (Psalms 32:3, 4).

The one who covers up his sin in this life is going to have it uncovered in the next, and whoever exposes it to God in this life shall never have it exposed again in the life to come. A day of judgment is coming. Jesus said, "Nothing is covered up that will not be revealed, or hidden that will not be known. Whatever you have said in the dark shall be heard in the light, and what you have whispered in private rooms shall be proclaimed upon the housetop" (Luke 12:2,3 RSV).

What this means, you see, is that a day is coming in which there will be absolutely no secrets, a day in which the disclosure of the heart will take place. For the godly, the disclosure will be rewarding; for the ungodly the disclosure will be damning. God will judge all sin that has been covered up; all sin that is hidden will be revealed. But the sin that is exposed and cleansed by the blood of Christ need never be exposed again. And the promise we have is that when we come to heaven, God is not going to show us our sins. But for the unbelievers who attempt to cover up their sins, the news is not so comforting.

Revelation 19 says that Christ will open the books to disclose the sin of their lives, He will judge all their sin, and He will cast the guilty into the lake of fire.

Now the reason that God is so stern in judging sin is that sin is always against Him. That was true even in the case of David who said, "Against thee, thee only, have I sinned, and done this evil in thy sight. . ." (Psalms 51:4). David was not denying that he had committed sin against himself and his own body, as adultery certainly is (1 Corinthians 6:18). He was not denying that he had sinned against Bathsheba and Uriah. He was not denying that he had sinned against the whole nation of Israel by failing in such a way. But he was recognizing that primarily all sin is first and foremost against God. Confession of sin is not just admitting that you did it, but it is admitting that you did it against God and that your sin was an affront to God.

That is one aspect of confession—agreeing with God that you are guilty. The Greek word is *homologeō,* meaning "to say the same thing." So when you confess your sin, you must agree with God that you are a sinner—that you see sin as He sees it. "Lord, I have sinned. I agree with Your estimate of myself."

But confession is not just saying, "Yes, I did it! I did it!" True confession also involves repentance, and repentance means turning away. You have not really honestly confessed your sins until you have stopped doing them. If a person says, "I'm sorry, God. I confess," and then continues to practice his sin, he is just fooling himself. So confession includes a brokenness in addition to a verbalizing, and brokenness leads to changes in behavior.

A Close Look at Confession.   Perhaps one reason why we make such surface confession is that we do not understand what is involved. We have an inadequate comprehension of the elements of confession. A closer look at David's Psalm 51, however, shows us that true confession involves a right view of sin, a right view of God, and a right view of self.

Right View of Sin.   What do we mean by a right view of sin? First, it is a recognition that sin deserves judgment. David prayed, "Have mercy upon me, O God, according to thy loving-kindness: according unto the multitude of thy tender mercies blot out my transgressions" (v. 1). The fact that David pleads for mercy is an admission that he is guilty and does not deserve exoneration or acquittal. The possibility of mercy comes only after the guilty verdict has been rendered.

Do you think David was taking a chance that he might not receive mercy? Then read Psalm 103 for great news! "The Lord is merciful and gracious, slow to anger, and plenteous in mercy. . . . For as the heaven is high above the earth, so great is his mercy toward them that fear him. . . . But the mercy of the Lord is from everlasting to everlasting upon them that fear him . . ." (vv. 8, 11, 17). We find many examples in Scripture where God stayed His hand of judgment and extended mercy, such as Ezra 9:13, Nehemiah 9:19, and: ". . . . Know therefore that God exacteth of thee less than thine iniquity deserveth" (Job 11:6). Although God eagerly grants us mercy, let us never forget that our sins deserve judgment.

A second aspect of a right view of sin is a recognition that it demands cleansing. David prayed, "Wash me throughly from mine iniquity, and cleanse me from my sin" (Psalms 51:2). David wanted every dirty sin washed out of his life. For one whose sin leaves a deep stain, only total cleansing will suffice. Let me point out something in this connection. Since David lived before the cross, his sin was covered but not removed. Each time he sinned, the cover came off, and he had to apply some more sacrificial blood to cover it up. Only in Jesus Christ can sin be permanently cared for. Those of us who put our faith in Christ were cleansed at the moment of conversion and made entirely clean. Then, as we walk in daily fellowship with Him, we are kept cleansed through the Word.

There is a third thing involved in a right view of sin—the matter of accepting full responsibility for it. David wrote, "For I acknowledge my transgressions: and my sin is ever before me" (v. 3). David did not blame anybody except himself. He says, in effect, "God, I exonerate You. I myself have done this. I have sinned. You are justified, You are clear. I don't try to escape my accountability." When a person is willing to take personal responsibility for his sin, then he is advancing toward spiritual maturity.

Last, a right view of sin recognizes that sin proceeds from one's nature. "Behold, I was shapen in iniquity, and in sin did my mother conceive me" (v. 5). I believe in genetic depravity—that sin is passed on from generation to generation at the time of conception. "The wicked are estranged from the womb . . ." (Psalms 58:3). From his earliest moment, man is evil. He cannot help it—it is a part of his very nature.

Right View of God.   Not only does true confession demand a right view of sin, but it also demands a right view of God. In Psalm 51 David cites several attributes and characteristics of God and draws practical applications from them. God's holiness, for example, requires "truth in the inward parts" (*see* v. 6). That implies that God is not concerned with external behavior but with the internal. Some people try to play games with God by carrying on a lot of external religious ritual. He is not impressed with that. God looks on the inside—at the heart.

David also referred to God's power: "Purge me with hyssop, and I shall be clean . . ." (v. 7). David expressed his confidence in God's power to take care of sin. Some Christians do not believe that God can change their sinful habits. I believe He can. But it requires trust and confidence in God's power to deliver. How often we fail to commit ourselves totally to Him for victory.

After holiness and power, David recognized God's chastisement. "Make me to hear joy and gladness; that the bones which thou hast broken may rejoice" (v. 8). Shepherds have been known to break the leg of a wayward lamb, and then to carry that little one close to their sides until the set bone has completely healed. After that, the sheep would follow the shepherd closely wherever he went. David got the message: "Lord, I had my legs broken, but now I'm ready to follow You."

One other aspect of a right view of God—His forgiveness. David knew God was a pardoning God, that He could and would forgive sin. I can think of no better expression of this than the verse found in Micah 7:18: "Who is a God like unto thee, that pardoneth iniquity, and passeth by the transgression of the remnant of his heritage? he retaineth not his anger for ever, because he delighteth in mercy."

Right View of Self.   True confession demands a right view of sin, a right view of God, and one thing more—a right view of self, as Psalm 51 also makes plain. David came to recognize that he must live a holy, godly life.

Why? First, for the sake of sinners. David knew that he must be holy if he was to convert other sinners to God (v. 13). No one is going to listen to a man who has a sense of guilt eating away at him and locking his lips from giving testimony. Such a one has nothing to say. I'm sure many Christians find themselves silent because they cannot avow the righteousness of God out of the context of a vile, unrighteous life.

Second, we must be holy for the sake of God who delights in a broken and a contrite heart (v. 17). Do you know that you can make God happy? You can—by being sensitive to sin and being broken before the Lord.

Last, we must be holy for the sake of the saints. In verse 18 David prays for others. He is back now on praying ground and he can intercede for others. But he could not do that unless he first came to that point of purity of life.

To summarize, true confession can only occur when you see God truly, when you see sin for what it is, and when you see yourself for what you are to be.

Why Confess?   Let me dispel a wrong idea which some people have regarding this matter of confession. In saying that confession involves both agreement with God and repentance that leads to sorrow for sin—does that mean we must beg God for forgiveness? The answer—an emphatic *no*. Why not? Because God has forgiven the believer's sin already! When Jesus died on the cross, He bore the sins of each believer—his past sins, his present sins, his future sins. So we are not dealing with the matter of forgiveness when we talk about confession. Forgiveness occurred at the cross. We can paraphrase 1 John 2:12 to read, "My little children, He has forgiven you all your trespasses for his name's sake." I do not have any unforgiven sin in my life. Neither do you, if you are a Christian. There is no such thing as unforgiven sin in the life of a believer. Colossians 2:13 states that God has forgiven us all our trespasses through our union with Christ.

I once saw a call-in television program dealing with religious themes. A woman telephoned in and asked, "If I die, or the Rapture occurs, before I have a chance to confess all my sins, what will happen to me? I'm a Christian." The expert responded, "You'll go to hell." Not so! All the sins of the Christian have been forgiven. This is what the cross accomplished.

The *why* of confession will be considered in the remainder of this chapter. I warn you—this is very heavy sea we are sailing through, so grab hold of the railing and hang on.

Clean! Clean!   We have to tackle three vital words, taking as our text 1 John 1:5–2:2. The first word is *cleansed.* "But if we walk in the light, as he is in the light, we have fellowship one with another, and the blood of Jesus Christ his Son cleanseth us from all sin" (1:7).

This is a fantastic description of a Christian. The word for *walk* is in the present tense subjunctive, which means it is continuous, habitual action—an index to character: *If you are habitually in the light.* Now who is that? The Christian who has been placed in the light—the Christian who is sharing God's common light and life. If you are in Him, then it follows that you are in the light.

The fact that Christians are always in the light is very clear in Scripture. God is in the light and no darkness is in Him. We are in that light also. This is an absolute. From the intellectual side, light refers to truth (*see* 2 Corinthians 4:4, 6; Acts 26:18, 23; John 12:35, 36, 46). From the moral side, light refers to holiness or purity (*see* Ephesians 5:8–14; Romans 13:11–14; 1 John 2:8–11). God is truth and holiness and no lie or sin touches Him. And we are in Him. What a thought!

Since you are walking in the light, you have fellowship "one with another." You might think that refers to other Christians, but it doesn't. It refers to God. That is not evident in the English text, but it is in the Greek. So as you walk in the light, you have fellowship with God. The word *fellowship* means "partnership." You are partners with God, sharing common life.

What is the result of this? *The blood of Jesus Christ His son cleanses us from all sin.* Let me explain. The blood is the symbol of the death of Christ. Peter uses it when he talks about being redeemed not with corruptible things such as silver and gold, "But with the precious blood of Christ, as of a lamb without blemish and without spot" (1 Peter 1:19). The blood symbolizes the Saviour's death which was completely efficacious for us— that is, it was on our behalf. And His blood shed at one time is a constant provision for our cleansing.

Revelation 1:5 also speaks to this point: ". . . Jesus Christ, who is the faithful witness, and the first begotten of the dead, and the prince of the kings of the earth. Unto him that loved us, and washed us from our sins in his own blood." When Jesus paid the price for sin by shedding His blood, that blood became like a cleansing agent and washed our sins away. It is not that the blood itself had some quality, but that the giving of His life paid the penalty for sin. And the giving of His life is symbolized in the shedding of His blood.

Any Catch?—Is there any condition attached to this cleansing? Yes, only one. You can be cleansed if you walk in the light. Now, walking in the light is simply being a Christian. If you are a Christian, then you have absolute, total, complete, continuous cleansing from all sin. That's what 1 John 1:7 affirms. There is no condition for cleansing but being in the light.

"No, no, you're wrong, MacArthur," someone objects. "This verse implies that we *ought* to walk in the light. It's saying, 'All right, you Christians, if you'll just get in earnest and walk in the light, then you'll have fellowship and then you'll be cleansed.'"

Okay, let's deal with the problem. If that interpretation is correct, then the verse, in effect, would be saying, "Don't sin, because if you do, you'll be in darkness." So let's read it that way: "If you don't sin, the blood of Jesus Christ will cleanse you from all sin." Well, that is not what we need. That would mean that cleansing is only for when you do *not* need it. Really, it wouldn't be of any value to you if you only got cleansed when you are already being good. Here the implication would be that cleansing and forgiveness are available only to those who don't sin.

No, instead the verse means that if you and I are walking in God's light when sin comes in our lives, we are nevertheless children of light, and sin is constantly cleansed from us because no darkness can invade God's light. And so God continually cleanses and cleanses and cleanses us because of the sacrifice of Christ.

I tell you—that's exciting! We don't have even one un-cleansed sin stacked upon another. Instead of being guilty and defiled, we are constantly cleansed. The moment that sin appears, we are cleansed because we are in the light. There is no darkness in Christ, and Christ keeps us pure.

Ephesians 1:7 tells us that one of the things we receive from Christ is "redemption through his blood, the forgiveness of sins, according to the riches of his grace." As rich as His grace is, that is how total our forgiveness is. And Hebrews 10:14 reminds us that the offering of Christ "perfected for ever them that are sanctified." His one offering led to our total cleansing, not just for one time, but for eternity as well.

I am fit to enter God's Holy Presence. I am going to glory nonstop! "To be absent from the body is to be present with the Lord" (*see* 2 Corinthians 5:8). Christians are always in the light, always in the fellowship, and always cleansed. Fantastic!

Let me give you an idea of how this works. On the occasion that our Lord washed the disciples' feet, He said, "He that is washed needeth not save to wash his feet, but is entirely clean: and ye are clean, but not all [all of you except Judas]" (*see* John 13:10). The one who is washed or who has taken a bath is totally clean. Yet back in the first century, as a man walked along the dusty road, his feet would get dirty. All he needed to do was wash his feet. That is what Jesus referred to. He is saying, "Once you have been cleansed, once you have been bathed, all sin has been forgiven. Only the dust of the world needs to be washed off your feet, and I will continue to do that. You don't need to be recleansed—to take another bath."

This wonderfully pictures the positional cleansing and holiness of the Christian at salvation and gives us the promise that Jesus will continue to keep us clean every day as we walk through the world. We do not need to be saved over and over again, but only once. Our salvation is a once-and-for-all experience.

Is It or Not?   So the first word to describe the believer is *cleansed*. Now let us return to our 1 John 1 text for the second word—*confession*. "If we confess our sins, he is faithful and just to forgive us our sins, and to cleanse us from all unrighteousness" (v. 9).

I have pointed out there was no condition for cleansing in verse 7, but now we are at verse 9. You see, verse 7 looks at the matter from God's side and verse 9 looks at it from our side.

"Well, there you are!" you may say, as you dig your elbow into my ribs. "You just said Christ takes care of our sins automatically, and now you're going to say that this verse says, 'If we confess. . . .' So there is a condition after all!"

No, not really. Let me show you what I mean. God forgives and cleanses because of the death of Christ. God does this instantly, but he does it only for the people who are confessing. You may read 1 John 1:9 this way: "If we are the ones confessing our sins, He is faithful to forgive our sins." Who are the ones who are confessing? Christians. Do you see it? This verse is not saying, "You must confess—or I will not forgive!" It says, in effect, that God constantly, habitually, forever cleanses the sins of the ones who are confessing. That is just another definition of a Christian. A Christian is someone who agrees with God that he is a sinner. So the ones who are admitting that they are sinners are the ones who are being cleansed.

Faithful and Just—Now notice that this verse says that God is *faithful* in this forgiveness. He is faithful because He promised that He would be. He promised that He would be merciful to the one who confesses (Proverbs 28:13). And in Jeremiah 31:34 He said, ". . . I will forgive their iniquity, and I will remember their sin no more." So God is faithful because He does what He promised.

But our text adds that God is *just* in doing this. How could

God possibly be just to forgive sin? Because Jesus Christ paid the penalty and, in doing that, He satisfied God's justice. Romans 3:23–26 tells us that our Lord was crucified in order to display the justice of God, so that we might know that God is just. And the justified are those who believe in Jesus.

Continuing—Often a look at the original language illumines a difficult point. When 1 John 1:9 speaks of *forgiving,* the word is used in the aorist, which is a form of verb referring to a single definite onetime act, rather than to continuous action. The Christian does not live in continuous sin, but individual acts of sin do occur and these need to be confessed.

The word *confess* is in the continuing present tense, which means that we are continually confessing our sins. It is not a onetime thing. Our confession must be continual and habitual. God keeps forgiving the ones who are confessing—the ones agreeing with Him that they are sinners. So the continuous habit of their lives is to be acknowledging before God that they are sinners. In doing this, a confessor shows himself to be the one who is being forgiven—a true Christian—in contrast to the non-Christian whose habit is to deny sin (*see* vv. 8, 10).

Let me illustrate this by looking at the word *faith.* You are saved by faith, right? Now, after you are saved, do you say, "I'll quit believing"? Of course not. In fact, if your faith is real, it will continue. Belief is not a onetime thing. The word *believe* is in the present continuous tense. Belief is a continuing act. It doesn't cease.

The King James Version of 1 John 5:1 sounds like a onetime deal: "Whosoever believeth that Jesus is the Christ is born of God. . . ." But it really means, "Whosoever continues to believe, whosoever habitually believes. . . ." That is what Jesus implied when He said, ". . . If ye continue in my word, then are ye my disciples indeed" (John 8:31). Again, "Who is he that overcometh the world, but he that [is continuing to believe] that Jesus is the Son of God?" (1 John 5:5). So if salvation is real, faith will go on.

Now, if the confession of sin that led to salvation was real, confession will go on as well. The things that brought you to

Jesus Christ—the acknowledging of your sin and faith in Him—will continue through your whole Christian life if you are genuine. This is what the Spirit of God is saying. Those who are saved will continue to believe and they will continue to confess. Perhaps I can sum it up in these four important words: CONTINUAL CONFESSION CHARACTERIZES CHRISTIANS.

Degrees of Thoroughness—I think there may be varying degrees of confession. Some may confess more frequently than others. There may be degrees in the fullness or completeness of repentance. But the same is true of faith, isn't it? Some have more faith than others. But Jesus said, "If you have faith of a grain of mustard seed, that's all I ask" (*see* Matthew 17:20). The point is that confession must be present, and as one grows in the Christian life, he will find himself confessing more often than when he first believed.

We really need to be honest in this area. The blessing of God is attended upon the confessing heart. We need to open ourselves before Him. If we have a superficial relationship with God, then our confession will be superficial—"Oh, Lord, I sinned again today and You know it. There are a whole lot of things I've done wrong, and I don't have time to go into them. Amen." Well, at least you admitted to being a sinner. You don't admit that you are much of one, but you're probably more one than you ever thought of admitting. How much more meaningful to truly acknowledge to God the depths of your sin—from the bottom of your heart.

Fellowship vs. Joy—Now some people say that confession is important because it restores the fellowship with God which has been broken by sin. You sin—fellowship is broken; you confess—fellowship is restored. But that is not so. Fellowship with God never changes. It cannot be broken by sin and therefore it cannot be restored by confession. We have been led astray—victimized, if you will—by the English usage of the word *fellowship,* which means friendship, intimacy, relationship between people. But the Greek word is *koinōnia,* meaning partnership. Our basic partnership with God can never be broken by sin. Something does happen when we sin, but it is not broken fellowship. It is forfeiture of joy. "These things I write unto you that your joy may be full" (*see* 1 John 1:4). Although your fellowship cannot be broken, you can foul up your life so that you lose your joy. Many Christians have done that very thing.

I don't deny that, in sinning, a believer loses a certain intimacy, a certain experience, a sense of warmth from God. Something does go away, but I define it as lost joy rather than lost fellowship. Now what is the fastest way to regain the joy of your salvation? To do what David did—to confess. "Restore unto me the joy of thy salvation . . ." (Psalms 51:12). God returns to you His joy.

Conquering.   So far we have seen that cleansing and confession characterize the Christian life. There is a third thing which the believer experiences—conquering. God liberates the Christian in that He gives the believer for the first time the ability to do what is right. That is something you never could do before you were saved.

"Who needs it?" a Christian may say to himself—or even aloud. "Since I'm going to be a sinner for the rest of my life and I have to keep confessing it, there's no need to strive for holiness —especially since I'm cleansed anyway. So I'll just live as I please."

John responds to that philosophy, "My little children [He's 90 years old when he writes, so he can use that expression.], I'm telling you these things that you sin not" (*see* 1 John 2:1). I like that! You will never hear a simpler exhortation than that: "People, don't sin!"

"Well, why did he say that? If I'm always going to be confessing and always going to be cleansed, isn't it ridiculous to say, 'Don't sin'?"

No, it isn't ridiculous, because you do not have to sin. That sounds like a contradiction, and, in a sense, it is. Within you lies the power for victory over sin, and that is why I use the word *conquering.* You can conquer sin. "For sin shall not have dominion over you . . ." (Romans 6:14). It has no more power over you. Romans 8:13 says you can "mortify" sin—you can kill it. Unbelievers cannot win over sin, but Christians can.

I believe with all my heart that one mark of spiritual maturity is the decreasing frequency of sin. Why would God say, "Sin not," if He didn't think you had the resources to do it? Paul said the same thing, "Awake to righteousness, and sin not . . ." (1 Corinthians 15:34). "Be ye angry and sin not . . ."(Ephesians 4:26). "For the grace of God that bringeth salvation hath appeared to all men, Teaching us that, denying ungodliness and worldly lusts, we should live soberly, righteously, and godly in this present world" (Titus 2:11, 12). In other words, we are not to sin. One of my sermons on Romans is entitled "Four Things the Holy Spirit Does for You Whether You Like It or Not." Among those sovereign works of the Spirit is the subduing of the flesh. *You* cannot conquer in your flesh, but the Holy Spirit working in you can.

On Your Side.   John closes with a brief summary: ". . . . And if any man sin, we have an advocate with the Father, Jesus Christ the righteous: And he is the propitiation for our sins, and not for ours only, but also for the sins of the whole world" (1 John 2:1, 2). John says, "in case you do sin, we have Somebody to cover." The writer is not speaking of a habitual action but of single acts. "If you happen to commit an act of sin, it is cleansed."

What is an advocate? It is the same word translated "Comforter" in John 15:26. It means a lawyer for the defense—someone called alongside to help. Whenever we sin, do you think that Love would accuse us? No, but Satan would. "Look at him, God. That child of Yours sinned." That is the prosecution.

But our Advocate, the Lord Jesus, comes up and says, "It is taken care of, Father, I bore it in My body. I took the penalty." So Satan is foiled. "Who shall lay any thing to the charge of God's elect? . . ." (Romans 8:33). Only a Righteous One could save us from all unrighteousness. Christ is holy and Christ made the perfect sacrifice.

There you have it. As those redeemed by our Lord Jesus Christ, we are cleansed. As cleansed ones, we confess our sins. And as those who confess, we conquer. No matter how deep your guilt, no matter how frequent your failure, come to God in contrite confession and let Him do His work in your life.

One of the most thrilling scenes in English literature comes at the conclusion of *Mutiny on the Bounty*. Some seamen are being court-martialed before the Royal Navy because of mutiny. Roger Byam, a young sailor, faces death with the others. The sentence is hanging, but because Byam is a person of loyalty and integrity, he is granted a pardon by the king. Though judged guilty, he is acquitted, restored to rank, and the record of his crime forever expunged.

That is what David asked for—and received. And that is what every believer receives in Christ. We believe God is a forgiving God, and in response and thanks, we confess to Him our sin, turning from it, lest we stamp on His grace.

6

Love—

Unlocking the Bridal Suite

At the time of Moses, God gave His people the Ten Commandments. But by the time of the Lord, the legal traditions of the rabbis totaled more than 600. Now there is no way for a person to perfectly keep 600 laws, so the Jewish leaders made an accommodation. They divided all their rules and regulations into heavy laws and light laws. "The heavy laws are just that," they said. "They're binding. The light laws? Well, you can give a little on those." Some rabbis even went further and taught that if a man selected just one great precept to observe, he could disregard all the others. Against this background, a lawyer came to Jesus with a question: "Master, which is the great commandment in the law?" (Matthew 22:36).

"Jesus said unto him, Thou shalt love the Lord thy God with all thy heart, and with all thy soul, and with all thy mind. This is the first and great commandment. And the second is like unto it, Thou shalt love thy neighbour as thyself. On these two commandments hang all the law and the prophets" (vv. 37–40).

Big Fisherman, Big Failure.   What is involved in keeping this first commandment which our Lord termed the greatest? I know of no better illustration than that furnished by one of the twelve disciples in John 21.

"I'm going fishing!" Peter said one day after the death and Resurrection of the Lord Jesus Christ. He was saying to the other disciples that he was going back to the fishing business— returning to what he used to do. Since Peter was the leader, the rest of the fellows said, "We're going, too," and they all went to the boat without any thinking on their part. The Lord re-routed all the fish in the Sea of Galilee. None went near the boat. So Peter and the others labored all night with nothing to show for it. (vv. 2, 3).

"Have you caught anything?" the Stranger called to them at the dawn of the new day.

"No," they answered.

"Cast the net on the other side of the boat and you will find." The Lord gave a supernatural whistle and the fish just stacked up on the right side of the boat. The catch was so big that the disciples couldn't even get them on board (v. 6).

"It is the Lord," John said. At that, Peter threw himself into the water and swam ashore (v. 7).

Jesus invited them to breakfast—a meal He had prepared, perhaps supernaturally. As Peter and the others sat there, eating with the Lord of Glory, Peter must have thought to himself, "What a clod I am! What a disobedient, inadequate person. I've failed again." Peter had failed every test given him. He just couldn't succeed. There must have been tears in his eyes and grief and pain in his heart as he looked at Jesus.

Love vs. Like. At last the Lord spoke: "Peter, do you love Me more than these?" (*see* v. 15).

These what? Well, maybe more than these things—the boat, the fish, the nets, the sea, the whole fishing business. Or perhaps the Lord was asking if Peter loved Him more than the other disciples did. Peter had claimed on one occasion that he did love more than the others, that he was more faithful than they.

"Peter, do you really love Me? Do you *super*love Me?" The Lord used the word *agapaō,* meaning the highest kind of supreme love.

How long Peter took in replying, we do not know. But at last he said, "Yes, Lord, You know that I love You." Only Peter used a different word—*phileō*—a word meaning, "I like You a lot."

I believe that Peter felt his love was supreme, but he could not claim that kind of love because of all his disobedience. It would have been ridiculous for him to say, "Lord, I supremely love You, but I don't do what You say."

I always remember once talking to a little five-year-old kid.

I asked him how he could show his parents that he loved them. "I could obey them," he replied. It is not right to claim supreme love if there is no obedience in the life. So Peter did not make this claim. Peter, you recall, had denied the Lord on three occasions, so Christ gave him three times to redeem himself. Jesus said to him a second time, "Simon, son of Jonas [The Lord called him by his old name because he was acting like his old self.], do you *super*love Me?" (*see* v. 16).

"Yes, Lord, You know I like You a lot."

Then Jesus probed a third time, only now he adopted Peter's word for love. "Simon, do you really like Me a lot?" The Bible says that Peter was grieved. Why? Because of being queried three times? No, because the Lord was questioning Peter's testimony, questioning the *level* of Peter's love (*see* v. 17).

"Lord, You know all things. You know that I like You." Peter was implying, "Don't hear what I say. Look at my heart."

When I was a little boy, I used to think about the doctrine of omniscience—the fact that God knows everything about everything—as a terrible problem. My dad used to warn me, "We may not know, but God knows! He sees what you do, Johnny." I wondered why God would waste His day just watching what I did.

As I matured in my understanding and grew up, I came to realize this—in many ways, I'm like Peter. And there are some days when the only way that God would ever know that I loved Him was if He *was* omniscient. And I realized that the doctrine had a positive side. Aren't you glad that on those days when your life does not make your testimony very clear that you can say, "Lord, I'm sorry about the way I act. Would You read my heart and know that I love You?" That's what Peter did.

The Quality of Loving God.   Now, what is the character of the kind of love that Jesus sought from Peter—that He seeks from us? Is it an emotional love—a sentimental, bumper-sticker kind of thing? Are we supposed to feel spiritual goose bumps toward the Lord? Well, there are times in my life when I don't jump up and down and feel this warm feeling toward Christ.

I just can't whip up that kind of reaction. But that is not what the Lord is talking about. We learn what real love is as we look further at this incident between Peter and Jesus.

Sacrifice.   "Peter, when you were young you put on your own belt and went where you wanted to go and walked where you wished. But when you get old, you shall stretch forth your hands, and another will bind you and carry you where you don't want to go. The Lord spoke this, signifying by what death Peter should glorify God" (*see* John 21:18, 19).

The phrase "stretch forth your hands" speaks of crucifixion. "Peter, you're going to be crucified. Peter, do you really love Me? Then die for Me."

This is what it means to love God with all your heart, soul, and mind. It is love willing to make a sacrifice of itself. That is not the sentimental kind of love we hear so much about. Peter had that already, but it wasn't enough. So now Jesus offered Peter a way to exhibit his love. He didn't just say, "Peter, does it feel nice inside to love Me? Do you feel kind of warm between your fourth and fifth ribs?" No, He asked for sacrifice.

How can you tell if you love the Lord Jesus Christ? It hinges on whether you are willing to make the ultimate sacrifice for His will as a daily thing. In the first century, sacrifice could very well mean physical death. The Roman General Varus reportedly put down an insurrection in Galilee by lining the road with crosses. Peter knew what his sacrifice would cost.

Now Peter had always sworn that he could handle this, but he remembered all his past failures. Yet here was the Lord making a flat prophecy that in the end Peter was going to be faithful. I think Peter must have said to himself, "Wonderful! At last—I'll make it! I'll stand true to the Lord. I won't fizzle out at the end."

Obedience.   There's a second quality to this love of which our Lord spoke. Not only is it self-sacrificial, but it is obedient. "Follow Me," the Lord commanded Peter. When Jesus got up and walked away, Peter arose and followed, literally interpreting this command. Yes, it is true that Peter digressed for a moment by turning, seeing John, and asking the Lord what lay ahead for the beloved disciple. "That's none of your business, Peter," the Lord said, in effect. And again He commanded, "Follow Me" (*see* vv. 20–22). Peter did—for the rest of his life.

What is involved in your giving sacrificial obedience to the Lord out of your love for Him? I can think of one thing it involves for myself. I spend five to six hours a day in my study, pouring over the Word of God. Quite frankly, however, on some days when I enter the office, I am tired and don't feel like studying. I would like to do something else—like dusting off the golf clubs and playing eighteen holes. But instead, I grit my teeth and struggle through a day of intense study. At the end of that day, the only emotion I feel is just the discipline of having done it. But in working, I have loved the Lord Jesus Christ over against myself. I have fulfilled His will and sacrificed in order to do it.

Now that may be a small thing—but it demonstrates the principle of sacrificial obedience. Such obedience out of love is not an emotional thing, but a fulfilling of 1 John 2:5—"But whoso keepeth his word, in him verily is the love of God perfected: hereby know we that we are in him." The love that God seeks— love of heart, mind, and soul—obeys.

Loving Others.   Now let's go back to our Lord's reply to the lawyer who asked about the greatest commandment. First, we are to love God, second we are to love others. Many Scriptures speak to this point. For example, 1 Thessalonians says that we have been taught of God to love one another. In view of that, we are to increase in love toward one another (4:9, 10). And Peter writes that we are to love one another with a pure heart, fervently (1 Peter 1:22). The word *fervent* comes from a Greek term meaning extended or stretched out. We are to stretch out as far as necessary to reach others.

Just as love for God is not an emotionally induced thing, neither is loving others. This also demands sacrifice. In writing about this, John switched from a statement about loving the brethren—plural—to loving a brother—singular (1 John 3:14). Some people say, "Well, I love the brethren—I just can't stand the individual brother." Sure, it is very easy to love the whole

wide world, and easy to love the church. It may be very difficult
to love one particular individual in the world or church.

Love by Deeds. When I first came to the church I serve, I
wanted badly to love everybody, but I couldn't figure out how
to get the emotional feeling that I thought was necessary. Some
people were kind of irritating and made things difficult for me.
I wanted to love them, but I didn't know how. But then one
day I went to one of these men, put my arm around him, and
said, "I want you to know something. If there's any way I can
ever serve you, I'd sure love to have the opportunity." The
opportunity came. I never felt any different about him emotionally, but I loved him by serving him.

Loving others is not a question of patting someone on the
back and saying, "You're so wonderful, so irresistible. I love
you!" The way we show love is to make personal sacrifices to
meet someone's need. Sometimes I'm asked how I can minister
to individuals in a large church. It is not by running around to
everyone and expressing love, but by making sacrifices in my
life for their maturing, as I help them to grow spiritually. I care
enough about them to do what is necessary in my life to bring
them into conformity to Jesus Christ.

How do we best know that God loves us? Has He ever
shouted it from heaven or written it in the sky? No, we perceive
the love of God because Christ laid down His life for us. God
put His Son on a cross on our behalf. That says it, doesn't it?
That is how He expressed His love—through sacrifice. And
since Christ laid down His life for us, we ought to give our lives
for the brethren (1 John 3:16). Our death may not be necessary.
"But whoso hath this world's good, and seeth his brother have
need, and shutteth up his . . . compassion from him, how
dwelleth the love of God in him?" (1 John 3:17). If we see
somebody who has a need, we must meet that need or we prove
ourselves to be deficient in love.

"Well," someone interjects, "before we can love somebody,
we have to love ourselves. After all, the Bible says we are to love
our neighbors as we love ourselves" (James 2:8).

I have heard many psychologists misinterpret that verse.

They say that you must have the proper self-image, that if you do not have an exalted impression of yourself and all that you are, you will never be able to love other people correctly. That is so much psychological gobbledygook. That stems from sentimental love, but the Bible speaks of something quite different.

What does it mean to love others as we love ourselves? Look at James 2:1—"My brethren, have not the faith of our Lord Jesus Christ, the Lord of glory, with respect of persons." And he goes on to give the illustration of a rich man and a poor man visiting a congregation and being treated differently. James is saying that as Christians we are not to treat certain people with respect while we treat others with indifference. Rather, to fulfill the royal law, we are to treat everybody as we would treat ourselves. That means that whatever great sacrifices we make for our own comfort, we should make for the comfort of others, without respect to their status in life. It has nothing to do with our psychological self, but it has to do with our service toward others.

Just stop, for example, and consider the lengths we go to make ourselves comfortable. That is the same way we should meet the needs of others. The way we treat our own desires, we should treat the desires of others. Love them in terms of self-sacrificing service, just as we make sacrifices for our own benefit. Are you willing to do that? Are you willing to give up whatever it is that makes you comfortable—to provide for the comfort of someone else? Are you willing to sacrifice the things you enjoy so that another's need may be met? This is loving your neighbor as yourself. It is not psychological, it is sacrificial.

Service Is Love.   I think the best example of self-sacrificing love for the brethren was given by our Lord Himself. On the night before He suffered and died, the Lord did not tell His disciples in the upper room, "I love you. I'd like to give you a discussion of divine love and tell you how it works."

Instead, "Jesus knowing that the Father had given all things into his hands, and that he was come from God, and went to God; He riseth from supper, and laid aside his garments; and took a towel, and girded himself. After that he poureth water into a bason, and began to wash the disciples' feet, and to wipe them with the towel wherewith he was girded" (John 13:3–5).

Following that amazing example of self-humiliation, Jesus said this: "A new commandment I give unto you, That ye love one another; as I have loved you, that ye also love one another. By this shall all men know that ye are my disciples, if ye have love one to another" (vv. 34, 35).

How had Jesus demonstrated His love for them? By washing their dirty feet, by taking the role of a slave, by doing the distasteful thing—the sacrificial thing. Loving each other is not just feeling little pangs of emotion. It is serving. When we willingly sacrifice what we want, for the good of another, when we choose to fill the need of someone instead of satisfying our own need, then we really love (no matter what our emotions may be). That is what God expects.

The Apostle John sums up love as a key to spiritual growth in simple and familiar words: "My little children, let us not love in word, neither in tongue; but in deed and in truth (1 John 3:18).

7

Prayer—

Unlocking the Inner Sanctum

Christianity is the hottest commodity in the universe! Yet most of us need to be constantly reminded of how fantastic the Christian life really is. All we have to do is to look at the Book of Ephesians. It tells us we are *super*blessed (1:3), *super*chosen (1:4), *super*accepted (1:6), and *super*forgiven (1:7). In Christ we are wise (1:8), rich (1:11), and secure (1:14). We are alive with new life (2:5). We are the objects of eternal grace (2:7). We are God's masterpiece (2:10) and close to God in a mystery kind of union both with Him and every other believer (2:13). We are one body (2:16) with access to God by one Spirit (2:18). We are the temple of God (2:21) and the habitation of the Spirit (2:22). And we are powerful (3:20).

What extraordinary statements. How great is the Christian life when examined as to what we are in Christ! We do not have to earn this exalted position because it is already ours through our salvation in the Lord Jesus Christ.

The last three chapters of Ephesians go beyond these positional aspects of our life and get into the practical aspects. Just for example—we are to walk intelligently as believers (4:17), to walk in God's love (5:2), and to walk in the light (5:8). This presentation of Christian adequacy has no rival in all of the Word of God. If any believer studies Ephesians carefully and concludes that he lacks something, he is mistaken. We do not need more of the Holy Spirit, more love, more grace, or more anything else. In Christ we have it all. We have everything we need to grow and to mature.

Warning: Danger Ahead! At this point, however, a potentially destructive problem arises. I call it spiritual overconfidence or doctrinal egotism. It is a latent danger in the Christian life that believers who have a very deep knowledge of doctrine and a fairly effective grip on practical spiritual principles become self-satisfied. And then heartrending, passionate, constant prayer finds no place in their lives. I have seen this very condition develop in life after life after life. Because of knowledge, a creeping self-dependence evolves which eliminates the vitality of a real prayer life.

To guard against this danger, Paul commands believers to "pray always." He summons us to a life of prayer. Regardless of how much we have in Christ, we must pray. Prayer is an essential key to spiritual growth.

For an analogy as to how necessary prayer is, think of the atmosphere and breathing. The atmosphere exerts pressure on your lungs and forces you to take it in. You breathe very naturally in response to this pressure instead of consciously going around grabbing for air. Since this is true, it is much more difficult to hold your breath than it is to breathe. You would never say, "Oh, I'm so tired today because I've been breathing." But you would be tired if you had been fighting not to breathe—fighting against the natural pressure exerted against your lungs.

The same is true in prayer. Prayer is the natural thing to do as a Christian. Prayer is the Christian's vital breath. The reason why some Christians are so fagged out and beat is that they are holding their breath spiritually when they should be opening up their hearts to God to accept the atmosphere all about them—His divine presence. The one who is not faithfully in prayer constantly struggles against his spiritual nature. He is holding his spiritual breath.

"Why would any Christian not breathe—not pray?" you ask. Good question. I think the answer is sin. Sin in our lives stifles prayer. When we are not willing to confess and to forsake it, we really do not want to pray, because prayer opens us up to God's presence, and we do not feel comfortable there.

In case you cannot think of any sin you do not want to admit, try this one on: selfishness. That is about the number-one reason why people do not pray. It manifests itself in symptomatic sins like laziness or unconcern or indifference. Look into your life and you can probably identify some sin that keeps you from prayer. And if you are not praying, you are suffocating. That is deadly!

The All*s* of Prayer.   In the last two chapters of Ephesians, Paul gives two brief but pointed emphases on prayer. The first is a general instruction and the second is a specific illustration. Each has a great lesson to teach. The general instruction is found in Ephesians 6:18: "Praying always with all prayer and supplication in the Spirit, and watching thereunto with all perseverance and supplication for all saints." Paul repeats the word *all* three times and uses the word *always* once. The same Greek word *pas* is used on each occasion. Taken together, these make up four different points regarding prayer. We might label them the *all*s of prayer.

How Often?   The first indicates the frequency of prayer: *praying always.* When should we pray? Someone says, "I think it's in the morning." Another insists, "I like to do it at night." Really? When do you breathe? "Oh, I take a few gasps of air in the morning."—"I get my air at night." How ridiculous! We must be praying always and always praying. The Greek construction means praying on every specific occasion.

I think Paul really meant this! And when our Lord Jesus said, "Watch ye therefore, and pray always . . ." (Luke 21:36), I think Jesus meant it, too. If our Saviour felt the tremendous desire and need to pray, knowing that He possessed His divine nature (*see* John 17), how much more strongly do *we* need to pray, even though we know our position in Christ?

The letters of Paul give us many commands as to the frequency of our prayers: " . . . continuing instant in prayer" (Romans 12:12)—"Be anxious for nothing, but in everything by prayer and supplication with thanksgiving let your requests be made known to God" (Philippians 4:6 NAS)—"Continue in prayer . . . with thanksgiving" (Colossians 4:2)—"Pray without ceasing" (1 Thessalonians 5:17). Paul not only talked it—he lived it. Paul constantly prayed for someone.

How is it possible to be always praying? First, we have to define our terms. To *pray always* means that we are God-conscious—that we see everything that happens with reference to God. Let me illustrate. You get up in the morning and look out on a beautiful day with a beautiful sky. What is your first thought? Perhaps it is, "Thank You, Lord, for this great day You have made." That is praying without stopping. Then you go outside and see your neighbor who is living in sin. So you pray, "God, save my neighbor!" More prayer without stopping. You get into your car and drive down a street and see signs advertising topless bars. You think in your mind, "God, what is this world coming to? God, help me reach those people who are lost and sick." Once again, you are praying without stopping.

Praying without end is not just reciting, "Now I lay me down to sleep," thirty-five times. It is seeing things with God's kind of viewpoint. It is seeing a hurt and asking God to heal it, or seeing a problem and asking God to untangle it. It is seeing a Christian brother who has a need and praying for him, or seeing a man in trouble and asking God to deliver him. It is communing with God about what you know is dishonoring to Him. All these exemplify what it means to pray without stopping. At every waking moment we are praising God for something wonderful or interceding for someone.

Count the Kinds. Paul also gives a second *all* of prayer—the variety in prayer—*praying always with all prayer and supplication*. Again, we must define our terms. *Prayer* is a general word pertaining to its many forms and character. For example, you can pray publicly, privately, verbally, silently. You can pray those deliberately planned prayers in which you open up a little prayer book, or you can pray those spontaneous prayers that just rip out of your heart. You can request something or you can give thanks. You can be kneeling, standing, sitting, lying down. There are many ways to pray—because God has designed prayer to go along with every kind of emotion and every kind of experience. We have a variety of forms of prayer to fit every situation and circumstance.

The second word Paul uses is to describe a particular type of prayer—*supplication*. That is best defined as a specific request. How often we generalize, "God, bless the missionaries. God, bless the church." Those are not specifics, they are generalities. Such vague requests are likely to lead to vague answers—if any at all.

My little daughter had a habit of generalizing. One night at the end of a long, tired day, she knelt by her bed and prayed, "God, bless everything in the world. Amen." I had to tell her that this was not a very good prayer. I had to conduct a little theological discussion to try to impress on her that God wanted her to tell Him specific things that were upon her heart, not "everything in the world." Supplication must be specific.

Keep an Open Eye.   Paul next considered the manner of prayer—*watching thereunto with all perseverance and supplication*. Perseverance means to stick at it. When you pray, stay with it—like that man in Luke 11 who kept banging away at the door until the storekeeper opened up to give him bread for unexpected guests who had arrived (*see* vv. 5–8). God says, in effect, that He will respond in similar manner. He listens for constant, persevering prayer.

A key word in this aspect of prayer is *watching*. That means to be alert. We cannot pray intelligently unless we are alert to what is going on. Many Christians forget or ignore Peter's plea to "watch unto prayer" (*see* 1 Peter 4:7). He urged us to sleepless, incessant, persevering, vigilant prayer.

Do you know what is going on in your home? What about your wife? Do you pray for her faithfully, without ceasing? Do you pray for her constantly, asking God to make her the kind of woman she ought to be? The kind of mother? The kind of wife? The kind of Christian servant God desires? Do you faithfully pray for her that God will bless her and enrich her life and bring her to spiritual maturity?

What about your husband? Do you pray that he might be

God's man in every sense of the word? Do you pray that he might be like Christ as he heads up the home? Do you petition God that your husband might make the right decisions? Do you pray that God will help him in his work? Are you aware of the problems and conflicts he is facing, and then pray about them?

What about your children? Do you pray that God will build them up in Spirit, that they will be strong in the Lord, that He will keep them from the evil one?

What about your neighbors? Those people around you? The kids at school? The sick? Those others who need your prayers? When someone shares a need, do you really pray or do you merely say, "Oh, yes, I'll pray for you," and then forget?

We used to have a man in our church who had in his bookcase a whole stack of notebooks of all the requests that he had prayed for and that God had answered through the years. At that time he was working on notebook number—(I don't recall how many.) This fellow was alert! When he heard of someone who had a need, he would write it down and pray—a great practice to follow.

I had a person tell me on one occasion, "MacArthur, I'm going to put you on my prayer list for six months." My first reaction was—"Boy, is that all I get?" But my second reaction was to praise the Lord. It is unusual to have someone commit himself to pray for you for a certain period of time. It is tremendous.

For Him, Not You. The fourth *all* that Paul speaks about concerns the objects of prayer. The *direct* object of our prayers, of course, is God. Paul said often, "We pray God. . . ." This suggests a very important principle which is stated clearly in John 14:13, 14. "And whatsoever ye shall ask in my name, that will I do, that the Father may be glorified in the Son. If ye shall ask anything in my name, I will do it."

Jesus was here comforting His disciples in their sorrow over His leaving. They were thinking how bad it would be without Jesus present to fill their needs, hear their cries, answer their requests, and protect them. After all, He had given them food, helped them catch fish, provided tax money, loved them, taught them, provided a shoulder for them to cry on. How could they survive without Him present to supply their needs? This promise which Jesus gave filled that void. Even though Jesus was to leave them, they would still have total access to all His supply for them. Prayer would remove the distance. What a promise!

There is, however, a condition which determines the Lord's response to prayer—*in My name*. What does this mean? Is it simply to tack on that phrase at the end of each prayer? No, it is much, much more.

First, it means to pray in His Person—that is, standing in His place, fully identified with Him, asking by virtue of our very union with Him. When we truly ask in Jesus' name, He is the petitioner.

Second, it means that we plead before God the merits of His Blessed Son. We are asking it to be granted for Christ. We desire it for His sake. When we truly ask in Jesus' name, He becomes the receiver.

Third, it means we pray only for that which is consistent with His perfections and that will be for His glory.

To pray in Jesus' name, then, is to seek what He seeks, to promote what He desires, to give Him glory. We can only rightly ask God for that which will glorify the Son.

So end your prayers with, "Father, this I ask because I know this is what Jesus would want for His own glory." Place that at the end of every prayer and you will have to eliminate all your selfishness. So the direct object is God. To Him and for Him we pray. Wow! This is practical!

Prayer for Others.   Next, Paul shifted to the *indirect* object of our prayers— *for all saints*. What compels us to pray for each other? For one thing, as members of the body of Christ we are all engaged in a common battle. "For we wrestle not against flesh and blood, but against principalities, against powers . . ." (Ephesians 6:12). We struggle to win victory through the name of Christ and to exalt Him by our lives. Since this is true, we have to expand our horizons above our own individual conflict and think in terms of the whole body of Christ. We are to be concerned not only for our own ultimate triumph, but for the spiritual victory of all other believers.

Often we think of ourselves as separate entities. So many times we get the idea that we exist independent of everyone else. But we don't. Just as the human body cannot make any forward progress unless all the members move, neither can the body of Christ.

Second, just as the body of Christ ministers through spiritual gifts, so we also minister through prayer. Is my spiritual gift of teaching for me? Should I take my spiritual gift and go off in a cabin somewhere and teach myself? Should I stand up in front of a mirror and preach to me? That is laughable. My spiritual gift is to be exercised for your benefit. Even so, the prayer life and prayer power that I have is not for me, either—it is for you. I am supposed to pray for you, and you, in turn, should pray for others.

God designed it that way for our unity. When one part of the physical body is hurt or sick, all the other parts come to its aid. If my eye is injured, my eyelid directly protects it, but indirectly the rest of my body functions to send healing to my eye. Similarly, if a brother has a need, you may minister to him directly through exercise of your spiritual gift or minister indirectly by praying. You know, I believe we would see great things happen if we really prayed for each other. Even though we enjoy an exalted position in relation to Christ, we still have a desperate need for the prayers of other believers. And likewise we need to be constantly asking God to work in specific ways for specific saints.

How do we get to know another's burdens and needs? That is a problem. Often nobody wants to share his burden. So we must take the initiative and open up a little and get to the place where we ourselves are willing to share. You will discover that someone else may have the same problem you do! So you could pray for each other. Face it—no one can possibly bear your burden if he does not know what it is.

That does not mean you have to tell everything to everyone else. That would be poor judgment. But let us at least start sharing our needs with those we know we can trust, and start praying for each other. That will take us out of spectator Christianity and get us into the arena where the struggle goes on. We need to remember that all of us are at war spiritually. If we really believe in the power of prayer, we will begin to pray and then to see God do things that otherwise He wouldn't.

Start Here!   All the above constitutes the instruction that Paul gave regarding prayer in Ephesians 6:18. But then he closes with an illustration, and that fits in with his usual pattern of teaching and then giving practical application. In this context, Paul follows the *all*s set forth in verse 18 with the specific example of verses 19 and 20: "And for me, that utterance may be given unto me, that I may open my mouth boldly, to make known the mystery of the gospel, For which I am an ambassador in bonds: that therein I may speak boldly, as I ought to speak."

What a man—this Paul! He laid down the principle and then said, "I'm the fellow you can start with!" Paul didn't ask for his physical needs—as we might have done—great as those were, but he requested prayer that he might possess the message of God and then have the courage to give it out. So the apostle was not asking for prayer selfishly; he asked that his ministry might continue unimpeded, even if he was in jail at the time. He uses himself as a living illustration, sharing his life with his readers in order that they might pray for him.

This sets a pattern of prayer for us. We are to be primarily concerned with the spiritual dimension. This means that instead of praying only for someone to be delivered from physical ills or trials, we should be praying that he would be in a right relationship with God so that he can relate to the trial with the proper attitude. Do not be so shortsighted that you stop praying for physical needs, but it is people's spiritual welfare which God is concerned with. Trial should bring growth. Paul's prayers were always in line with spiritual objectives, physical ones were never the issue.

As you learn to pray as Paul instructs, you will find yourself becoming God-conscious and selfless. And as you humble your-self, spend time with the Holy Spirit, and pray under His super-vision, you will find your life being melted and molded into the very image of Jesus Christ. And that's what it is all about!

8

Hope—

Unlocking the Hope Chest

Hope—one of the greatest words of the Christian vocabulary! Paul, writing to the Corinthians, said, "These three things are the greatest: faith, hope, and love, and the greatest of these is love" (*see* 1 Corinthians 13:13). Here we have a triad of Christian virtues—and one of them is hope. Spiritual maturity must include a strong hope.

The very word itself shines like light in darkness—joy in sorrow, life in death. You can imagine how it must be for people in the world who have to live with false hope or with no hope. Hypocrites have a false hope. They are erroneously counting on being secure in death, counting on heaven, counting on a happy afterlife. But the Scriptures say, "For what is the hope of the hypocrite . . . when God taketh away his soul?" (Job 27:8). So some have false hope in religion, as others maintain useless hope in gold or silver.

Then there are people described in the Bible as having no hope. The pagan world is said to be without hope and without God (Ephesians 2:12). Look at the heathen philosophies in Paul's day and you can readily understand why. Some believed that the soul, temporarily imprisoned in the body, would one day reluctantly leave through the last gasp of breath or through an open wound. The soul would then enter Hades (or the grave) —the shade world—and it would spend the rest of whatever eternity was left bemoaning its existence without comfort of any kind. Theognis said, "I rejoice in sport in my youth; long enough beneath the earth shall I lie and so be voiceless as a stone, leaving the sunlight which I love. Good man though I am, then shall I see nothing more." That is hopelessness—a hopelessness without God.

Now any honest, objective person—anyone who did not escape through drink or drugs—would find it almost impossible to live in hopelessness. Men must have a confidence in the future if they are to survive the present.

Romans 8:24 speaks to this issue so far as Christians are concerned: "For we are saved by hope: but hope that is seen is not hope: for what a man seeth, why doth he yet hope for?" This verse suggests that not everything in terms of our salvation can be referred to in the present tense. The fullness of our salvation is a hope for the future.

Count the Ways.   While we could not begin to investigate all that the Bible says about hope, let us look at some of the general statements. First, the Bible says our hope is to be in God and in God alone. The only secure place for hope is in Him. In Psalms 43:5 we read, "Why art thou cast down, O my soul? and why art thou disquieted within me? hope in God: for I shall yet praise him, who is the health of my countenance and my God."

Then, too, the Bible tells us that hope is a gift from God—a gracious gift. "Now our Lord Jesus Christ himself, and God, even our Father, which hath loved us, and given us everlasting consolation and good hope, through grace" (2 Thessalonians 2:16). Now this is a benediction, but it makes for a beginning and a middle as well. God grants to man hope, confidence, assurance, security for the future—all this if we accept His gift.

"Where do I get this gift?" you ask. The Bible says that hope comes through the Scriptures. When you read the Word of God, when you understand the Word of God, and when you believe the Word of God, then you have hope. "For whatsoever things were written aforetime [that is, the Old Testament] were written for our learning, that we through patience and comfort of the scriptures might have hope" (Romans 15:4). If you do not believe the Book, you are hurting for hope. But for confidence in the future, trust the Word.

A fourth thing may be said about hope—the fact that it is secured by Christ's Resurrection. If God were merely to say, "You can trust Me in death, I'll take you through," that would be sufficient. But we have an even stronger hope when we see Christ go through death and come out on the other side. He has conquered death. "Blessed be the God and Father of our Lord Jesus Christ, which according to his abundant mercy hath begotten us again unto a lively hope by the resurrection of Jesus Christ from the dead" (1 Peter 1:3).

Hope is further confirmed in us by the Holy Spirit. "Now the God of hope [one of His names] fill you with all joy and peace in believing, that ye may abound in hope, through the power of the Holy Ghost" (Romans 15:13). One of the ministries of the Holy Spirit is to convince the believer that he has hope for the future. That knowledge acts as a tremendous defense against Satan as he tries to shake us up about the future. Without hope we might begin to get shaky. But hope defends us against Satan and his lies.

For more on this, think of 1 Thessalonians 5:8 which talks about the Christian's helmet—the hope of salvation. Satan comes along with his great big broadsword and wants to split your confidence wide open. But you simply remember that the Spirit of God has confirmed to you, by the Resurrection of Christ, the gracious gift of God—hope. So the sword bounces off your helmet with no injury to you.

Let me point out something else about hope. Hope is to be continual. Among the many passages speaking to this is Psalms 71:14: "But I will hope continually, and will yet praise thee more and more."

Another wonderful thing about hope is that it produces joy. "Happy is he that hath the God of Jacob for his help, whose hope is in the Lord his God" (Psalms 146:5). Why is he happy? Because hope brings joy.

Is it necessary to point out that hope removes the fear of death? When we really hope in God, when we hope in Christ our Saviour, there is nothing to fear. Colossians 1:5 refers to the hope laid up for you in heaven. We know that God has a future for us; we know that He has a promise for us; we know that we have hope for the future because the Lord Jesus lives in us now! Our Lord's Resurrection is the basis for this hope, the removal of our fear of death.

Another thing that may be said about hope is that it is secure. Nothing need ever take away our confidence, need steal away our hope. Hebrews 6:17, 18 say that our strong consolation and the hope set before us rest on two immutable things—the fact of God's promise and the fact of God's oath. In other words, our hope is secure because God made the promise and underscored it with an oath.

When will our hope be fulfilled? When Jesus comes. "Looking for that blessed hope, and the glorious appearing of the great God and our Saviour Jesus Christ" (Titus 2:13). At the return of the Lord—that's when hope will be finally realized.

Hope of the Believer.   We could not leave our consideration of this theme without looking at 1 John 2:27–3:3, one of the great passages on hope. We discover in this section five features of the believer's hope.

The believer's hope is guaranteed by abiding.   When John talks about abiding, he is talking about being saved—about a permanent remaining in Christ, which is the measure of a true believer. That concept goes back to the Lord's words: "If you continue in my word, then you are my disciples indeed" (*see* John 8:31). True disciples continue.

What is to insure that the believer will abide? Not *what*, but *who*—the Holy Spirit. A paraphrase of 1 John 2:27 might read, "The Holy Spirit has been given to you, and He will abide in you so that you don't need any human teachers, but as the Holy Spirit teaches you all things and is truth and is no lie, even as He hath taught you, you shall abide." The Holy Spirit is an internal lie detector. The Holy Spirit is a resident truth teacher. He dwells within every Christian to prevent him from ever forsaking the truth.

Now we come to verse 28: "And now, little children, abide in him. . . ." What John is really implying is—"Be real. Be true believers. Be Christians." Those who let the Gospel abide in them will abide in the Son and in the Father and in the Spirit and so they will continue in Christ.

Cooperate—We are not absolved of responsibility. Many verses in Scriptures say, in effect, "Here is what God has done for you, now you go out and do it yourself." (Compare Jude 21 with v. 24; John 17:6 with 2 Timothy 4:7.) Privileges in the Scripture never cancel obligations. They only increase them. While our abiding in Christ is insured by the Holy Spirit, we are not released from accountability.

When the Spirit is given to us, that is not to exempt us or to make us irresponsible. It is not to make us indifferent, but to make us more diligent and more faithful—to hold tighter to those things that we know to be true. We are to discipline ourselves to conform to the Spirit's work and His will in our lives. When the Bible says we are to walk in the Spirit, it means to behave ourselves commensurate with the working of the Holy Spirit in our lives.

For example, the Lord said to Peter, "But I have prayed for thee, that thy faith fail not . . . " (Luke 22:32). That did take care of Peter, but a few verses later, the Lord looks the disciples in the eyes and says, "Pray that you enter not into temptation" (*see* v. 40).

In 1 Corinthians Paul says, "Saints, don't worry. God is faithful, and He will not suffer you to be tempted above that ye are able, but will with the temptation make a way of escape, that you may be able to bear it" (*see* 10:13). They might have said, "Great! God will make a way out of it. God will take care of our problems. God is in control." But then the next verse says, ". . . flee from idolatry." That's another paradox. The inward working of God's grace never sets aside exhortation. Don't ever accept the sovereign working of God in your life as an excuse for indolence, inactivity, or nondiscipline.

When He Comes—Now let's go back to our text in 1 John, and read further: "And now, little children, abide in him: that, when he shall appear, we may have confidence, and not be ashamed before him at his coming" (2:28). That is a tremendous statement. There is not going to be one Christian abiding in Christ who is going to be ashamed when Jesus comes back!

The mistakes in our lives will be taken care of in the blood of Christ. The word *confidence* literally means boldness. Jesus is coming and you can be bold when He gets here. Revelation 22:12 says, "And, behold, I come quickly; and my reward is with me, to give every man according as his work shall be." Jesus comes to reward His church for our service.

This is thrilling! Let me show you some verses to explain what is called the *Bēma* or Judgment Seat of Christ. "For I am now ready to be offered," wrote Paul, "and the time of my departure is at hand. I have fought a good fight, I have finished my course, I have kept the faith: Henceforth there is laid up for me a crown of righteousness, which the Lord, the righteous judge, shall give me at that day . . . " (2 Timothy 4:6–8).

What day? The day when Jesus is manifest to His church. Paul adds to verse 8: "And not to me only, but unto all them also that love his appearing." They love it so much they serve Him. They are believers, they are Christians, they are abiders. And they will be bold in getting their reward.

Rewarded—Check 2 Corinthians 5:10. "For we must all appear before the judgment seat of Christ; that every one may receive the things done in his body, according to that he hath done, whether it be good or bad." The King James Version of the Bible uses the words *good or bad*, but the real meaning is "useful or worthless."

To understand that, we have to look at a long parallel passage in 1 Corinthians 3: "For other foundation can no man lay than that is laid, which is Jesus Christ. Now if any man build upon this foundation gold, silver, precious stones, wood, hay, stubble; Every man's work shall be made manifest: for the day shall declare it, because it shall be revealed by fire; and the fire shall try every man's work of what sort it is. If any man's work abide which he hath built thereupon, he shall receive a reward. If any man's work shall be burned, he shall suffer loss: but he himself shall be saved; yet so as by fire" (vv. 11–15).

"Wood, hay, stubble" does not seem to refer to sin. Those are, rather, the useless things you do which have little consequence. They are not bad, just useless. All this neutral stuff will go up in smoke. The only things left will be those attitudes and actions that were totally for Christ, and for those you will receive a reward. Your positive things will be rewarded.

Since this is true, we ought to be very slow in trying to judge the works of others. That is not our job, it is His. "Therefore judge nothing before the time, until the Lord come, who both will bring to light the hidden things of darkness, and will make manifest the counsels of the hearts: and then shall every man have praise of God" (1 Corinthians 4:5). What is every single individual at the Judgment Seat going to have? Praise from God. So when Jesus comes, those of us who abide are going to have confidence when we see Him—confidence because Christ has taken care of our sin, burned up all the stubble, and has left only something for which we can be rewarded.

The word *confidence* literally means outspokenness or freedom of speech. It is the same word which is used in Hebrews, which invites us to come boldly before the throne of grace, and the same boldness we have in prayer (1 John 3:5). The same boldness, that same confidence with which we enter the holy of holies by the blood of Christ allows us to walk to the Judgment Seat of Christ without shame because we are abiding in Christ.

Of course, when Christ is manifest, there is going to be much shame in people who did not abide in Christ, who were not believing. To find out just how ashamed they will be, read Revelation 6:15: "And the kings of the earth, and the great men, and the rich men, and the chief captains, and the mighty men, and every bondman, and every free man, hid themselves in the dens and in the rocks of the mountains; And said to the mountains and rocks, Fall on us, and hide us from the face of him that sitteth on the throne, and from the wrath of the Lamb: For the great day of his wrath is come; and who shall be able to stand?"

The key to this is found in Mark 8:38. Jesus said, "Whosoever therefore shall be ashamed of me and of my words in this adulterous and sinful generation, of him also shall the Son of man be ashamed, when he cometh in the glory of his Father with the holy angels." Who's going to be ashamed when Jesus comes? The people who were ashamed of Him and of His words in this age.

Blameless—True believers—those who abide in Christ—are not going to be ashamed. In fact, they will be blameless. First Corinthians 1:8 tells us that we shall be confirmed "unto the end, that ye may be blameless in the day of our Lord Jesus Christ." Not only that, we are not going to have even a spot or wrinkle to mar our appearance (Ephesians 5:27). Fantastic!

Do you need more proof? Colossians 1:22 says that Christ suffered death "to present you holy and unblameable and unreproveable in his sight." First Thessalonians 3:13 says, "To the end he may stablish your hearts unblameable in holiness before God, even our Father, at the coming of our Lord Jesus Christ. . . ." We have a great hope, and this hope also is guaranteed as we abide in Christ. That is the first major point John wanted you to observe.

Our hope is realized in righteousness. It is made real or visibly genuine by our pattern of life. Look at the next verse of our text: "If ye know that he is righteous, ye know that every one that doeth righteousness is born of him" (1 John 2:29). John uses two different Greek words here translated *know.* The first means to know absolutely, the second to know by experience. So he is saying, "If you know as an absolute that God is righteous, then you know by experience that everybody that does righteousness is born of Him."

God is righteous, meaning He is innocent of any evil at all. He always does right things and makes right judgments. Since He is that way, you would expect that His children would behave similarly. Children tend to be like their parents. The people who really have this hope will not be righteous and blameless at the *Bēma,* they will be righteous now because they are born of God. So if our hope is genuine, it will be realized in a righteous life.

First Peter 1:14 adds something to that: "As obedient children, not fashioning yourselves according to the former lusts in your ignorance." He says Christ is coming back and you ought to be obedient. You should not act as you did before becoming Christians. So Peter immediately adds, "But as he which hath called you is holy, so be ye holy in all manner of conversation. Because it is written, Be ye holy for I am holy" (vv. 15, 16). You can tell a child of God because he acts as a child of God should act. Further, Paul said, "Examine yourselves, whether ye be in the faith . . . " (2 Corinthians 13:5). How would you examine yourself? You would look at your works, at your fruit. So our hope is realized by a righteous life. True hope will result in holy living.

Our hope is established by love.   Back to our text—1 John 3:1: "Behold, what manner of love the Father hath bestowed upon us, that we should be called the sons of God: therefore the world knoweth us not, because it knew him not." Love gave us our hope.

I used to wonder to myself, "Couldn't John come up with something better than *what manner of love?*" How about super, colossal, stupendous, magnanimous, unbelievable love! Then I realized that John was simply overwhelmed and astonished. He must have been saying to himself, "I can't believe that God loved me so much that He made me His child. It would be far more than I deserve just to be His slave. It would not have been half-bad to be His neighbor, and would have been great to be called His friend. But to be His son! I can't get any closer than that!" John just couldn't handle it. The concept was too great.

Out of This World—Look further at that expression "what manner of love." In classical Greek the words *what manner (potapos)* speak of a foreign race, country, or tribe. So John is saying, "What kind of foreign love did God bestow on us to make us His sons?" In other words, the love of God that made us sons is foreign to the human race, outside the human realm, unearthly, otherworldly. It belongs in another dimension.

Let us illustrate the use of this phrase further. In Matthew 8:23–27 Jesus had a small problem—a storm at sea while He was asleep. When the disciples awoke Him and cried out, "Save us, we perish," Jesus arose and rebuked the winds and the sea. He stood up and said, "Quiet!" "But the men marvelled, saying, What manner of man is this, that even the winds and the sea obey him?" (v. 27). Same word. "Where did Jesus come from? What kind of unearthly, otherworldly person is this?" They used it of Jesus, and John used it here of God's love.

One further illustration—in 2 Peter 3:10, 11 the apostle said, in effect, "Seeing then that you know about the Second Coming, how everything's going to be dissolved and the elements will melt with fervent heat, and the works that are in it are going to be burned up, and the Lord is going to come like a thief in the night—seeing that you know all of this, *what manner* of persons ought you to be?"

Listen, if you are God's child and you know how it is all going to end, you ought to be that same kind of otherworldly, unearthly kind of person. Do you want to attach yourself to something that is going to be burned up? Jesus was an unearthly Person, and we are to be unearthly people.

Human vs. God's Love—Now the word *love* in 1 John is *agape*. It, too, carries the idea of being unearthly. Human love is object oriented. In other words, it selects a nice object and loves it. Human love discriminates on the basis of the object. But God's love has nothing to do with the object. God's love is based on God's nature. And that is a foreign, unearthly kind of love outside our experience. God loves you, not because you attracted His love, but because it was His nature to love and you happened to be in existence. So you got loved! Tremendous!

The result of God's wonderful love is that we should be called the children of God. It is exciting to realize that God is my Father. He is not just my great God somewhere off in the distance; He is near and He loves me. I can go to Him as I can to my human father and know that if I ask Him for bread, He is not going to give me a stone, because He loves me. I am His child. In fact, He has even promised that I am a joint heir with Jesus Christ, His Son. Everything He has prepared for Christ, He is going to let me share!

The parable of the Prodigal Son illustrates this very well. After he had squandered his inheritance, recognized his sin, and returned home, did his dad treat him as a slave? No, as a son. God made you a son, not a slave. Your relation to Him is that of a child to a loving Father.

John is saying in this text: "This whole confidence, this whole hope I have in the future is based on the love of God—an unearthly love, an otherworldly love, a love beyond what humankind could ever conceive." Then he adds, "No wonder the world doesn't know us because it doesn't know Him." Jesus said that we should not be surprised if the world hates us because it hated Him (John 15:24). Christ was otherworldly. So are we. But how exciting!

Our hope is fulfilled in Christ's likeness.   Imagine that! Someday you are going to be like Christ. "Beloved, now are we the children of God" (*see* 1 John 3:2). When did you become a child of God? The minute you believed. Are you a child of God now? Absolutely.

Of course, you are not crowned as yet. You still have to struggle with mortal weakness and the devil's crowd. But you are no less a son of God. It is just that God is not finished with you yet. He is a Sculptor who keeps chiseling away, as the form He desires emerges. Michelangelo said once, "In every block of stone I see an angel to be liberated." God looks at each of us and says, "There's something in there and I'm going to get it out."

What is a continuing process now will become an instantaneous accomplishment when Jesus comes. The last part of verse 2 reads, " . . . and it doth not yet appear what we shall be: but we know that, when he shall appear, we shall be like him; for we shall see him as he is."

Note the three steps: first, He will appear, then we shall see Him as He is, and finally we shall be like Him. This is His plan for us. God is going to make every Christian like Christ. Check

Romans 8:29: "For whom he did foreknow, he also did predestinate to be conformed to the image of his Son. . . . " That is exciting—to know that we will be like Him! John 17:23 promises it as does 1 Corinthians 13:12. But the promise of all promises about seeing Jesus comes to us in Revelation 22:4. "And they shall see his face; and his name shall be in their foreheads." We are going to see Jesus face to face for all eternity, and when we see Him we will be transformed into becoming like Him.

The verse says we will actually be like Christ. So does Philippians: "We look for the Saviour, the Lord Jesus Christ, who shall change our lowly body that he may fashion it like his glorious body" (*see* 3:20, 21).

The post-Resurrection appearances of our Lord give us suggestions as to what His glorified body is like. It could pass through walls, could appear and reappear as He chose. He ate in His body. He could instantly fly to places—to the mountains, right up to heaven. That is the way we will be.

First Corinthians 15 gives us a great deal more information about our future glorified bodies. They will be incorruptible, meaning no decay, no growing old, no falling apart (v. 42). Our bodies will be glorious, transcending anything we can imagine, and will be powerful, with all weakness forever behind us. The bodies God will one day give us will be spiritual—that is, governed by spirit, not by animal life (v. 43). The kind of body Christ now has, we shall one day share.

Our hope is characterized by purity.   "And every man that hath this hope in him purifieth himself, even as he is pure" (1 John 3:3). If you really have this hope and you know you are going to be like Christ, it should change the way you live.

You see, our hope is not just theological—it is ethical. It has behavioral consequences. If I really believe in the coming of Christ, if I really believe that He is going to reward His church, if I really believe that He is going to bring me to His Judgment Seat, then this belief is going to make a big difference in the way I behave.

In the Apostle John's day—as in ours—there were people who were saying, "We're Christians! We're Christians!" But a look at their lives disclosed no purity, no righteousness, no love, no obedience. So John declared, "Write them off! They're wolves in sheep's clothing. They're phonies." The proof of being a Christian is not just having a hope; the proof is having a hope that makes a difference in the life.

The knowledge that you will one day be like Christ should motivate you to become like Him now. We are creatures of motivation, and this is certainly the highest motive to make us live lives that are pure.

When I used to play football, everybody had to do push-ups at the end of practice sessions. We would—so long as the coach watched. When he turned his back, however, we would be tempted to lie on the ground. But if he glanced again in our direction—back to action! The very presence of an authority figure changed the way we behaved. That is external motivation.

Jesus is not coming back simply as an authority figure. He is coming back as a loving Saviour who desires to reward us and to make us like Himself. That should motivate us internally to love and obey Him and to conform ourselves to the purity that is His standard.

Keep at It.   There will be times in your Christian experience when you will feel like giving up, quitting, climbing out of the arena of life. When that happens, think of that little group of believers—suffering persecution and tribulations—to whom Paul wrote. He reminded them that they had been called " . . . to the obtaining of the glory of our Lord Jesus Christ" (2 Thessalonians 2:14). He urged them to stand fast on the Word of God.

Then Paul added this benediction in which I would like to join: "Now our Lord Jesus Christ himself, and God, even our Father, which hath loved us, and hath given us everlasting consolation and good hope through grace, Comfort your hearts, and stablish you in every good word and work" (vv. 16, 17).

Hang on to hope!

Conformity

Oh, to be like Thee, dear Jesus, my plea,
Just to know Thou art formed fully in me.
On with Thy beauty, Lord, off with my sin,
Fixed on Thy glory Thy likeness to win.

Oh, to be like Thee, Thine image display,
This is the Spirit's work day after day.
Glory to glory transformed by His grace,
Till in Thy presence I stand face to face.

Oh, to be like Thee, Thou lover of men,
Gracious and gentle compassionate friend.
Merciful Saviour, such kindness and care,
Are only mine when Thy likeness I share.

To be like Thee, Jesus!
To be like Thee, Jesus!
For this I live, to this I'll die;
It is my hope, my prayer, my cry.

J. F. M., Jr.